Jesus Christ
the Apple Tree

*Reflecting on the many ways
of seeing Jesus*

ANTHEA DOVE

First published in Great Britain in 2007

Society for Promoting Christian Knowledge
36 Causton Street
London SW1P 4ST

British Library Cataloguing-in-Publication Data
A catalogue record for this book is available from the British Library

ISBN 978–0–281–05961–4

1 3 5 7 9 10 8 6 4 2

Typeset by Kenneth Burnley, Wirral, Cheshire
Printed in Great Britain by Ashford Colour Press

Produced on paper from sustainable forests

This book is dedicated to:

Daniel O'Leary, whose words were its inspiration,
Chris and Eilish Heath, faithful friends,
Helen Douglas, my role model,
Brendan Walsh, who makes me laugh,
and as always, to my husband, Chris.

Contents

Foreword

I have always loved the carol, 'Jesus Christ the Apple Tree'. It is old; it may have been written in the eighteenth century but it is more likely to be medieval. I like it because it seems such a strange metaphor for Jesus, and because it conjures up pictures of this lovely tree, so pretty in its springtime blossom, so beautiful hung with ripe fruit in autumn and so endearing in winter, especially when it is old and gnarled, its lower branches leaning down towards the grass, inviting young children to climb and play. I wonder why the writer saw Jesus as an apple tree. We can't know, for all the imaginings of painters through the centuries, what Jesus looked like, but we do know that in mind and spirit he was beautiful. We know also that he was indeed fruitful, that his words have inspired millions of people all over the world, often to change their lives.

So the carol celebrates the beauty and fruitfulness of Jesus. It has made me want to look at the gospel stories afresh, and made me seek out what are for me the powerful qualities of the person Christians believe to be the Son of God. It has inspired me to love and worship him in a new way as I have tried to discover what he was really like.

This book consists of my sometimes wandering, sometimes focused thoughts as I have tried to develop my understanding of who Jesus was, and is, to discover my own 'apple tree', my own image of this complex man who was both human and divine. I realize that this is a very personal quest, and that each of us will experience Jesus differently, but I hope that my musings may help to throw some light on ways of seeing the one who was born to be king, to suffer grievously and to change the world.

I should say at the outset that meditating on Jesus in this way has made me realize not only how human he was, but how he is alive in humanity. There is a sense in which he *is* the leper, *is* the woman suffering from a haemorrhage, in which he *is* the frightened deportee forced to return to a land where he will be tortured and killed, *is* the young woman dying of cancer. He is not a separate superior being looking on with compassion while we suffer; he is in the heart of our pain.

Jesus Christ the Apple Tree

The tree of life my soul hath seen,
Laden with fruit and always green:
The trees of nature fruitless be
Compared with Christ the apple tree.

His beauty doth all things excel:
By faith I know, but ne'er can tell
The glory which I now can see
In Jesus Christ the apple tree.

For happiness I long have sought,
And pleasure dearly I have bought:
I missed of all; but now I see
'Tis found in Christ the apple tree.

I'm weary with my former toil,
Here will I sit and rest awhile:
Under the shadow I will be,
Of Jesus Christ the apple tree.

This fruit doth make my soul to thrive,
It keeps my dying faith alive;
Which makes my soul in haste to be
With Jesus Christ the apple tree.

(From *Divine Hymns or Spiritual Songs*,
compiled by Joshua Smith,
New Hampshire, 1784)

Jesus – beauty

First, staying with the apple tree, I will consider Jesus and beauty. We know from St John that Jesus was there 'in the beginning'. He was, with his Father, co-Creator of the universe. Many of us, not only Christians but those of other faiths, particularly the ancient Celts and the Native American Indians, are and have been moved to worship God through the beauty of Nature. Gazing at a sky ablaze with stars or at a primrose, breathing in the scent of honeysuckle or freshly mown grass, listening to the song of a blackbird or the chuckle of a mountain beck, feeling the tickle of grass on our bare feet or stroking the cheek of a newborn child; tasting the sweetness of honey or the seductiveness of fine wine: all these can fire our senses to adore the Creator.

The poet Gerard Manley Hopkins found beauty in God's creation, and here especially in the oddity and quirkiness sometimes to be found in Nature:

PIED BEAUTY

> Glory be to God for dappled things –
> For skies of couple-colour as a brinded cow;
> For rose-moles all in stipple upon trout that swim;
> Fresh-firecoal chestnut-falls; finches' wings;
> Landscape plotted and pieced – fold, fallow, and plough;
> And all trades, their gear and tackle and trim.
>
> All things counter, original, spare, strange;
> Whatever is fickle, freckled (who knows how?)
> With swift, slow; sweet, sour; adazzle, dim;
> He fathers-forth whose beauty is past change:
> Praise him.

Yet it is not enough to praise and thank God because he created all the beauty of Nature. He is the ground of our being and we praise and thank him because the holy Spirit of Jesus is *in* all that is lovely, *in* all that moves and inspires us.

A CHILD'S INSIGHT

Lord Jesus, I saw you in that little flower
the one I nearly trampled underfoot.
I picked it, and held it in my hand, and looked at it
and saw that it was beautiful
and saw it was a violet
and knew that it was you.

* * *

Jesus – newborn

The Incarnation is the moment when God, in Jesus, became human, took on himself all the attributes of humanity, our flesh, our pain, our sweat and tears and temptations, our laughter and our joy. It was the moment when he identified with you and me, when the newborn child in the manger became like other babies, who, as now, are born into very different circumstances.

The infant Jesus, a newborn child, is lying in a manger. He is vulnerable, naked and weak. He looks like any other Jewish baby, and like any other baby he speaks to the tenderness of women. His mother and father will protect him, clothe him against the cold, feed him and cradle him. He is utterly dependent on them, for security and for life itself.

*

In Zimbabwe, at Christmas, a baby girl is born. They call her Sipiwe, and she lies on the hard mud floor. She is vulnerable, naked and weak. She looks like any other Zimbabwean baby, and there is nobody to feel tender towards her. Her mother is dying of AIDS. Her father is dead. There is no-one to clothe her, protect her, feed her, cradle her. She is utterly dependent, and soon she will die.

*

In the stable at Bethlehem, the infant Jesus is crying because he is hungry. At once his mother gives him her breast, and now he sucks contentedly. Her milk will make him healthy and strong. After feeding, Jesus falls into a peaceful sleep.

*

In a shanty town outside Lima a newborn child is crying from hunger, but there is nobody around to hear Antonio. His mother is away, somewhere in the city, struggling to earn enough to keep her family alive. Antonio is thin. It is easy to count his ribs. Flies buzz around his beautiful dark eyes. When will his mother come? When will he stop crying?

*

Jesus, the Son of God, the holy child, is poor. His bed is a trough where cattle feed. He is dressed not in finery but in swaddling clothes. He does not know it yet, but he will grow to love the poor, and to identify with them.

*

The baby girl, Anastasia, was born in Kensington, London. She is rich. She lies in a beautiful cradle, specially made for her by a craftsman. Her clothes are made of the finest cotton, patterned with exquisite embroidery and trimmed with lace. She sleeps with a fluffy pink teddy bear. A mobile, of stars and fairies, dances over her head.

*

When he is a few weeks old, the baby, Jesus smiles for the first time. Soon he laughs for sheer delight. His mother and father respond with joy. They hug and caress him and they are filled with wonder.

*

When baby Tyson, born in Hackney, London, smiles for the first time, no-one notices. His mother is doing her best to stay clean after years of heroin and crack cocaine. She is sitting in front of the television trying to stop shaking, and smoking non-stop. She hasn't looked at Tyson for hours.

*

The infant Jesus is threatened. He is in danger from a man in power who is so desperate to hold on to that power that he is willing to murder innocent children. His parents must flee to a foreign land, and he has become a refugee.

*

Somewhere in the Congo, a newborn child is threatened. He is in grave danger. Outside his hut men are rampaging, men with guns and machetes. One drags the baby's father from the hut. Two men enter and rape his mother before they kill her. The baby is left to die.

*

What is the point of all these comparisons? They attempt to illuminate the truth that Jesus Christ, even from the instant of his birth, was essentially human. He was God made flesh, born like all of us, though without sin. And because he was so truly human, his life was bound up with all of humanity. The other babies described were, each of them, his brother or his sister. Disease, hunger, poverty, danger and luxury are all part of the human condition, so while we sing carols and look at idealized paintings of the Christ-child, it is good to remember the other children too.

Jesus was (and is) God, but he also belongs to the family of humanity. When he grew up, he always cared in the depth of his being for the poor, the hungry, the oppressed, for all the marginalized people of the world. He touched the leper, he blessed the children, he told what is arguably the greatest story ever told, the story of complete forgiveness we call 'The Prodigal Son'. Perhaps we cannot kneel before the manger and adore the holy child without also paying homage to all the 'little ones' who suffer.

Before the manger, whether it is an actual representation of the Nativity, a crib in a church or at home, perhaps, or in our imagination, Christians for centuries have been drawn to worship the Christ-child. Meditating, we find ourselves asking, like the nineteenth-century poet Christina Rossetti:

> What can I give him,
> poor as I am?
> If I were a shepherd
> I would give a lamb.
> If I were a wise man,
> I would do my part,
> yet what I can I give him,
> give my heart.

*   *   *

Jesus – humility

On the third day there was a wedding in Cana of Galilee, and the mother of Jesus was there. Jesus and his disciples had also been invited to the wedding. When the wine gave out, the mother of Jesus said to him, 'They have no wine.' And Jesus said to her, 'Woman, what concern is that to you and me? My hour has not yet come.' His mother said to the servants, 'Do whatever he tells you.' Now standing there were six stone water-jars for the Jewish rites of purification, each holding twenty or thirty gallons. Jesus said to them, 'Fill the jars with water.' And they filled them to the brim. He said to them, 'Now draw some out, and take it to the chief steward.' So they took it. When the steward tasted the water that had become wine, and did not know where it came from (though the servants who had drawn the water knew), the steward called the bridegroom and said to him, 'Everyone serves the good wine first, and then the inferior wine after the guests have become drunk. But you have kept the good wine until now.' Jesus did this, the first of his signs, in Cana of Galilee, and revealed his glory; and his disciples believed in him.

John 2.1–11

What do we learn about this man Jesus from the story of the wedding at Cana? What kind of person does he show himself to be? We can guess the following with reasonable certainty: he is someone who is reluctant to reveal his power, who respects and defers to his mother, who is concerned for his hosts, who knows about wine and is happy to be at a party.

This story is about a miracle and about a marriage, but what stands out for me is the humility of Jesus, this man who had so much power within him but hesitated to use it and when he did, acted discreetly so that his host would not be embarrassed and so that no-one would single him out for praise. Jesus nearly always shuns the limelight after he has performed a miracle or a healing. Perhaps this was sometimes for fear of the Jews, but it seems that he never sought a position of power for himself.

True humility is a hard-won virtue and often false humility is part of the show we put on for the world, part of the disguise we wear in the hope of approval, affirmation and success. So, if someone expresses admiration for our appearance, our achievements or our personality, we rush to deny them. If a friend remarks: 'How pretty your hair looks!' a common response is a shrug and a falsely humble remark like 'It needs washing.'

The writer of Psalm 139 has no truck with such pretence. With joyous gratitude he cries to God: 'I thank you for the wonder of my being.' Those who, like Jesus, are truly humble, work quietly in the background, not seeking praise but happily accepting any affirmation that comes their way. It is easy to imagine that after the wedding party, Mary would have congratulated Jesus and thanked him and perhaps laughed with delight, remembering the pleasure of the wedding.

There is a passage attributed to St Paul in his letter to the Philippians, which is poetry rather than prose. It is a powerful depiction of the humility of Jesus.

> Let the same mind be in you that was in Christ Jesus,
> who, though he was in the form of God,
> did not regard equality with God
> as something to be exploited,
> but emptied himself,
> taking the form of a slave,
> being born in human likeness.
> And being found in human form,
> he humbled himself
> and became obedient to the point of death –
> even death on a cross.
>
> Therefore God also highly exalted him
> and gave him the name

that is above every name,
so that at the name of Jesus
every knee should bend,
in heaven and on earth and under the earth,
and every tongue should confess
that Jesus Christ is Lord,
to the glory of God the Father.

Philippians 2.5–11

And there is another short and moving piece of writing which conveys the essence of humility in a man who was universally despised in his world, an 'untouchable'. The words, Buddhist in origin and anonymous, reveal the gentle dignity of a human person to whom no respect had ever been shown.

A BUDDHIST POEM

He who is Blessed passed by my hut,
passed me, the barber.
I ran and he turned, waited
for me, the barber!
I said, 'May I speak to you, Lord?'
He said, 'Yes.'
Yes, to me, the barber!
I said, 'Can your Peace be for a person like me?'
He said, 'Yes.'
His Peace for me, the barber!
I said, 'May I follow you, Lord?'
He said, 'Yes'
to me, the barber!
I said, 'May I stay close to you, Lord?'
He said, 'You may.'
Close to me, the poor barber!

Anon

*   *   *

Jesus – clearsight

The next day Jesus decided to go to Galilee. He found Philip and said to him, 'Follow me.' Now Philip was from Bethsaida, the city of Andrew and Peter. Philip found Nathanael and said to him, 'We have found him about whom Moses in the law and also the prophets wrote, Jesus son of Joseph from Nazareth.' Nathanael said to him, 'Can anything good come out of Nazareth?' Philip said to him, 'Come and see.' When Jesus saw Nathanael coming towards him, he said of him, 'Here is truly an Israelite in whom there is no deceit!'

John 1.43–47

Jesus knew at once that Nathanael was 'a man incapable of deceit'. We might comment, 'It takes one to know one', because of course the description applies equally to Jesus himself.

Nathanael (aka Bartholomew) was a rare individual. I ask myself how many people I know are truly incapable of deceit. Sadly there are very very few, if any.

Most of the 'Nathanaels' I have met are not grown-up, mature men and women, they are not even among the old and the wise. No, in my experience, the 'Nathanaels' are people with learning difficulties or very young children, too young to be 'people-pleasers'.

'Nathanaels' have an innocence which makes them see clearly, see beyond superficiality and pretence. I think of Annabel and Liam, who both have Down's Syndrome. Neither of them would or could act from an ulterior motive. With Liam and Annabel, what you see and hear is what you get.

And although it happened a long time ago, I remember how my daughter Pippa taught me to at least try to see with the clear eyes of innocence.

You were with me that day, Pippa,
you were three years old.
Outside the bus shelter people were gathered,
angry, disgusted people.
A stranger sat in the shelter,
dirty and dishevelled,
a pool of urine at his feet,
a bottle of purple liquid on the bench beside him,
his hair matted,
his eyes dead.
People turned up their noses.
'He stinks' said one.
'It ought not to be allowed' said another.
I was listening to them,
talking with them and nodding.
I didn't notice when you slipped your hand from mine
and approached the repulsive stranger.
Then the bus came –
Horrified, I grabbed you,
but you looked back, so I looked back
and saw the light in his eyes
before we walked away.

*   *   *

Jesus – acceptance

As Jesus was walking along, he saw a man called Matthew sitting at the tax booth; and he said to him, 'Follow me.' And he got up and followed him.

And as he sat at dinner in the house, many tax-collectors and sinners came and were sitting with him and his disciples.

When the Pharisees saw this, they said to his disciples, 'Why does your teacher eat with tax-collectors and sinners?' But when he heard this, he said, 'Those who are well have no need of a physician, but those who are sick. Go and learn what this means, "I desire mercy, not sacrifice." For I have come to call not the righteous but sinners.'

Matthew 9.9–13

Matthew the tax-collector, whom Mark and Luke call 'Levi', was a sinner. In Palestine in the days of Jesus, the words 'tax-collector' and 'sinner' were synonymous, because taxmen cheated the people and took enough money for themselves to make them rich.

But there was something so compelling about Jesus that he only had to invite Matthew to follow him and he dropped everything and came to Jesus at once. There followed a party; Jesus enjoyed a meal, eating and drinking with Matthew and the sort of companions considered unsuitable by the Pharisees.

Jesus was never judgemental; on the contrary he welcomed and befriended sinners.

On New Year's Eve, Anna asked her teenage children to come with her to church. 'There couldn't be a better way to see in the New Year, could there?' she asked. Fourteen-year-old Toby wanted to please his mother and agreed to accompany her, but Jessie, aged 17, declared that she was going to a party. Anna stayed up long after midnight, worrying about her daughter, dreading that she might come home drunk or worse. About two o'clock Jessie turned up, not drunk, but a little merry, and not alone.

A smaller girl Anna had never seen before hung back behind Jessie. She was wearing a shabby overcoat that was much too big for her, and she was looking down at the floor.

Jessie threw her arms around Anna in an exuberant hug. 'Happy New Year!' she said, then, 'Mum, this is Penny. She's got nowhere to sleep. She's homeless. I said you'd be glad to let her sleep here. That's right, isn't it?'

*   *   *

Jesus – a learning curve

Jesus left that place and went away to the district of Tyre and Sidon. Just then a Canaanite woman from that region came out and started shouting, 'Have mercy on me, Lord, Son of David; my daughter is tormented by a demon.' But he did not answer her at all. And his disciples came and urged him, saying, 'Send her away, for she keeps shouting after us.' He answered, 'I was sent only to the lost sheep of the house of Israel.' But she came and knelt before him, saying, 'Lord, help me.' He answered, 'It is not fair to take the children's food and throw it to the dogs.' She said, 'Yes, Lord, yet even the dogs eat the crumbs that fall from their masters' table.' Then Jesus answered her, 'Woman, great is your faith! Let it be done for you as you wish.' And her daughter was healed instantly.

Matthew 15.21–28

When we read the story of the Canaanite woman's encounter with Jesus for the first time, most of us tend to be disturbed and dismayed. Can he really have behaved and spoken like this? Gentle, tender, loving Jesus? Of course we can make excuses or allowances: 'Matthew couldn't possibly have remembered his exact words . . . the comment about house dogs wouldn't have had the same effect as it would on us today . . .' But we have to be truthful, and admit that something isn't quite right here.

Jesus was without sin, and he committed no sin on this occasion, but he was a man of his time, and although his attitude towards women was remarkably more enlightened than that of his contemporaries, certainly at the beginning of his ministry he shared views which we would now consider prejudiced.

It is important to remember that like every other human being, Jesus changed and matured as he got older. We read in St Luke's Gospel of the child Jesus, that he grew in wisdom and stature. So he was not born 'perfect' but continued to learn wisdom. He listened and took on board the views of this foreign woman who was instrumental in teaching him, in opening his eyes.

Today attitudes are different. In most democracies discrimination against people because of their race, gender, sexuality or beliefs is acknowledged to be wrong. But we all have to go on learning, to be open to new attitudes.

John always prided himself on his relationship with his two sons, Robert and Michael. And he knew he had been a good father, spending a lot of his leisure time with them. Like him they had both grown up to be good sportsmen, and he felt a lot of this was due to the long hours he had spent teaching them to swim, and watching them playing football and tennis.

Now they had left home and were embarked on successful, rewarding careers. When Michael was in his early twenties he came home one weekend, and in the evening, after supper, he told his parents that he was gay. His mother smiled and hugged him and asked if he had a partner. His father said nothing, but the look on his face was enough. From that day he spoke to Michael only when he had to. He was coldly polite, whereas he made no attempt to hide his delight and interest in Robert.

John sometimes felt guilty about his attitude towards Michael, and although his wife, Anne, never made any comment, he suspected that he was a stick-in-the-mud, unfairly prejudiced against his younger son. Yet somehow, ever since what he thought of as 'the boy's revelation', he simply could not extinguish his feelings of revulsion and shame whenever he looked at Michael.

John was a retired army officer and he had always been very careful never to associate in any way with homosexuals: that was a matter of pride. But he also felt deeply ashamed that a son of his had turned out like this. He could see that Michael was the same pleasant, cheerful, good-natured fellow he had always been, but whenever he felt like 'weakening' in his stern disapproval of the young man, he steeled himself to stiffen his resolve.

Then, three years later, to the sorrow of the family, Anne became terminally ill. They were all extremely sad, but John was devastated.

Overnight he seemed to crumble; the old soldier who always stood erect and looked you in the eye became a pathetic old man.

Anne hated being in hospital; she begged John to let her die at home. He was distressed and bewildered; he knew he wouldn't be able to cope. Robert, the elder son, saw his father's dilemma.

'Don't worry, Dad,' he said, 'I'll pay for Mum to be in the best nursing home we can find, and you can visit her every day.'

'Hang on a minute, Rob,' said his brother, 'there's no need for that. I'll look after Mum. I'll give up my job for a while and take care of her.' John had never experienced what it is to have tears fill your eyes, at any rate not since he was a small boy, but now he had to turn away and pretend to be blowing his nose.

In the weeks that followed, he watched Michael's patient, sensitive care for his mother. Not content with basic nursing, he brought her flowers, and when she had no appetite, her favourite foods. She could no longer read or watch television, but Michael played the music she liked, and sometimes read to her.

Several times, John wanted to say something, to praise Michael, to thank him, to show his appreciation, but he didn't know how to begin.

Anne's illness was brief; she died peacefully one morning with John and both her sons at her bedside. The following day, Robert gently approached the subject of the funeral, and John said he would like to discuss and plan it that afternoon. The three of them chose hymns and readings and Robert, who was a headmaster and used to organizing things, remembered all the details. He was also accustomed to speaking in public, and he said to his father: 'I think one of us should say something in the church about Mother and our memories of her.'

John didn't answer for a moment. He looked at his two sons, feeling a strange mixture of pride and humility. Then he smiled at them both, and said, 'Yes, that's a very good idea. Would you like to do that for us, please, Michael?'

*　　　*　　　*

Jesus – self-effacement

When John heard in prison what the Messiah was doing, he sent word by his disciples and said to him, 'Are you the one who is to come, or are we to wait for another?'

Jesus answered them, 'Go and tell John what you hear and see: the blind receive their sight, the lame walk, the lepers are cleansed, the deaf hear, the dead are raised, and the poor have good news brought to them.'

Matthew 11.2–5

Jesus was never boastful, conceited or showy. He could have used John's question to show off, but he believed that it was God, working in him and through him, who was transforming the bodies, minds and hearts of the people he encountered in his healing and teaching. So he did not say, 'I am the one who has given sight to the blind . . .' etc.

When I think about people I know who are, like Jesus, self-effacing, I think of my friend Shirley who was my neighbour for a number of years. Shirley had left school, without passing any exams, at the age of 16. She had worked in a factory until she married Jim and her life was taken up with being a wife and mother – and, incidentally, a very good neighbour.

But by the time she was in her mid-forties, all three of Shirley's children had left home and she decided it was time to look for a job. She soon realized that finding work was going to be difficult. All that was on offer for someone as unqualified and unskilled as Shirley was work as a cleaner or a barmaid or back in the factory where she had started.

None of these appealed to her, and she was beginning to feel disheartened when her eye caught an advertisement in the local paper for a care assistant in an old people's home. Shirley went for an interview and the matron took one look at this healthy, clean, bright-faced and earnest middle-aged woman and hired her on the spot. Shirley turned up the next day, 'ready for anything' as she said, and was surprised to find that all her co-workers seemed younger than her own daughters. Then when she went into the big communal room of the home she was shocked.

About a dozen old people, mostly women, sat in a semi-circle facing a television set, though none of them seemed to be actually watching the programme that was being shown. Some had their eyes closed, and there was no animation in the faces of those who were awake. In that first instance, Shirley told me, she resolved, 'I'm going to change things around here!'

It didn't take long. Shirley made sure that she did all that was asked of her thoroughly and quickly and then devoted the rest of her time – and often a great deal more – to getting to know each resident. She talked to them and listened to them. She brought in photos of her own children to show them and admired all those she was shown. She arranged for a friend to play and sing for the residents once a week, and, when and if she could, brought in their favourite sweets, records or books. She came in laden with flowers from her garden and in short did everything she could to brighten the residents' lives.

The old people's home was transformed. Of course this did not go unnoticed. Some of the young carers were impressed and began to follow Shirley's example, often working overtime for nothing and bringing in small gifts to cheer the residents. But others didn't like it. They didn't like Shirley. They thought her 'goings-on' might mean that they would have to work harder. Worse than this, they knew that the assistant matron's post would be coming up shortly, and they were afraid that Shirley, who had only been at the home a comparatively short while, would be given the job. Soon after this Matron summoned Shirley to her office and offered her the post. To her surprise Shirley shook her head and said, 'Oh, no, Mrs Bentley, I couldn't.'

'Nonsense! You certainly could. You're by far the best worker I've had since I've been here. You've completely changed the atmosphere of this place and all the residents love you.'

But Shirley shook her head again. 'No, I'm sorry, I can't do it!'

Mrs Bentley was disappointed and bewildered. 'But whyever not?'

'Well, I know it would mean a lot of paperwork and admin – the sort of thing Edna has to do [Edna being the retiring assistant matron], and I couldn't bear to have less time with the residents. I don't need more money and I don't want to be important. I just want to try to help them to be as happy as they can be.'

*   *   *

Jesus – surprise

He entered Jericho and was passing through it. A man was there named Zacchaeus; he was a chief tax-collector and was rich. He was trying to see who Jesus was, but on account of the crowd he could not, because he was short in stature. So he ran ahead and climbed a sycomore tree to see him, because he was going to pass that way. When Jesus came to the place, he looked up and said to him, 'Zacchaeus, hurry and come down; for I must stay at your house today.' So he hurried down and was happy to welcome him. All who saw it began to grumble and said, 'He has gone to be the guest of one who is a sinner.'

Luke 19.1–7

Jesus surprised the people around him when he invited himself to the hated tax collector's home. Some of them were shocked and angered. But often we need to be made to think, to be challenged about our attitudes. Surprises, even painful ones, can be good for us.

This story reminded me of something that once happened to me, and I tell it aware that it shows me in a bad light. I had been made a governor of a school for disabled children which was run by Roman Catholic sisters, and I decided to invite the head-mistress, Sister Columba, for tea at my home. I liked and admired her a lot, and I wanted her to think well of me. I thought she might have been impressed by my kindness in inviting her, and I hoped she would like my nice home.

Knowing that nuns live a simple life, devoid of luxuries, I decided to make it a tea for her to remember. I made a gooey chocolate cake and meringues oozing cream. The day before Sister Columba was due she telephoned to ask if she could bring a couple of children with her. Of course I said yes, but I was a bit disappointed. I had been looking forward to an in-depth conversation, just the two of us. Since being appointed a governor, I had only visited the school briefly and glanced into the reception class where I had seen some sweet little children in wheelchairs listening attentively to their young teacher.

So it was a big surprise when Sister Columba drove up to my house and I saw two children in the back of her car. They were both girls, both large adolescents. One of them was grinning at me. She was firmly strapped into a special seat, but her whole body was shaking and out of control. I didn't see the other one properly at first, but when the nun, a fragile woman of amazing strength, lifted her out of the car, I was even more dismayed. In contrast to the other girl, she was quite limp, her head hung down so that I could only glimpse her face, and she was dribbling and making peculiar noises.

Sister Columba was smiling. 'This is Charlotte,' she said. 'Could you take her while I get Grace out?'

Very awkwardly, I took Charlotte's weight in my arms, at the same time struggling in vain to stop her dribble landing on the crisp new blouse I had put on specially for this occasion. Somehow the four of us got into the house and into the sitting-room. What followed was a nightmare for me. I wrote earlier that I wanted this to be a tea Sister Columba would remember; certainly it was a tea I would never forget.

There was chocolate cake and dribble on my best linen napkins, Grace's leg suddenly shot out causing one of my best china cups to fall and break, Sister Columba couldn't prevent Charlotte from peeing on my Persian rug, and worst of all, she made so much noise that Sister and I could hardly exchange a word. I was praying for it all to be over.

At last Sister Columba got to her feet. I saw that her habit, spotless when she arrived, was now smeared with chocolate and cream.

'I'm so grateful to you,' she said. 'These two hardly ever get invited anywhere. It's been such a treat for them.'

I was stricken with shame, and perhaps it was at least partly as a result of that tea-party that I gave up being a governor and went to work in the school instead.

*   *   *

Jesus and relaxing

One sabbath while Jesus was going through the cornfields, his disciples plucked some heads of grain, rubbed them in their hands, and ate them.

Luke 6.1

I suppose if I had a passion for darts or playing the harp or met-alwork and I read in the Gospels that Jesus was engaged in the pastime that brought me joy, I would momentarily and illogically feel happy to know this. So it was for me when I read that Jesus went walking through the cornfields with his friends.

I very much enjoy walking in the hills near my home. I could call such a walk 'an occasion of prayer' because over and over again my heart lifts in praise and thanksgiving to the source of such loveliness: our God. The songs of the skylark and blackbird, the sight of wild flowers, trees, mountains and hills, playful becks and deep rivers, the smell of honeysuckle and freshly cut grass: all such things draw me to worship him.

This very day I went for a walk. It is the middle of March, and in my part of England the snowdrops are beginning to wilt. The sun was shining, clouds raced across the high blue sky, the wind blew cold from the north-west. Everywhere in the little dale there was a sense of expectancy. The hedges were just on the verge of turning green, the wild daffodils that grow in such profusion along the banks of the stream were about to burst into flower, and any moment now the heavy slow-moving ewes will be suckling their newborn lambs.

Walking is such a great joy for me, but not only because Nature is so beautiful. When I walk with a companion we are sometimes content to be silent; at other times there is an opportunity to converse in depth as we stroll along. It is much easier to open up and share our innermost concerns with a friend while walking with him than it is when we confront each other from armchairs.

At one time I had the privilege of working with young people, and sometimes we were able to take them away for a weekend. Then we would go for walks in pairs, and find this an opportunity for sharing our fears and hopes and dreams in a way that might not have been possible in other circumstances.

I wonder if Jesus sometimes took just one disciple with him for a walk, Thomas perhaps, or Nathanael or Judas. What might he have learnt and understood about each of them, and how deeply would their lives have been enriched by such a personal, liberating encounter?

*　　　*　　　*

Jesus and pomposity

They do all their deeds to be seen by others; for they make their phylacteries broad and their fringes long. They love to have the place of honour at banquets and the best seats in the synagogues, and to be greeted with respect in the market-places, and to have people call them rabbi.

Matthew 23.5–7

When my parish priest comes into church on a Sunday morning, I sometimes feel like laughing. I happen to know him as a friend, and a less pompous, less self-regarding man you couldn't hope to meet. Except on Sundays in church, he is to be seen in clothes that are clean but casual and informal. He dislikes being addressed by any other title than his Christian name.

On Sundays, instead of solemnly processing, he hurries rather awkwardly into the church almost as though he hopes not to be noticed. But of course all eyes are upon him. It is his job to preside over the celebration of the service.

I feel like laughing because to those of us who know him the garment he has to wear seems so incongruous. He stands there, as he would say, 'dolled up in this ridiculous get-up'. It is unquestionably beautiful, a long flowing cream-coloured robe in heavy fabric, parts of which gleam like satin. It is embroidered all over with silken thread, the colours varying according to the season: gold, silver, purple, green or blue; and it is as far removed, we can guess, from the garments worn by Jesus Christ as can be imagined. When one chasuble was taken to be dry-cleaned, it was listed as 'evening gown'!

Why do the majority of our Anglican and Roman Catholic hierarchies still insist on the wearing of such elaborate and costly garb for their priests? Their answer to this inquiry would probably be: 'We do it for the greater glory of God.'

This same phrase is also used to justify elaborate and costly churches. I admit that I would be one of the first to complain if the authorities decided to discontinue the upkeep of our wonderful churches and cathedrals. But I complain much louder when I hear that a new church is being built or a large, old, not especially beautiful one repaired. Surely it is wrong to spend large amounts of money on such enterprises when the number of churchgoers is dwindling and, more importantly, when there is such an opportunity for the people of different traditions to share a building for worship, so giving true practical witness of Christianity.

As for the greater glory of God, I suspect he is glorified wherever there are acts of humility, compassion, justice and truth.

*   *   *

Jesus and home

Those who love me will keep my word, and my Father will love them, and we will come to them and make our home with them.

John 14.23

I feel somehow stunned when I read this, and am conscious of my complete unworthiness to be a home where God may dwell. I feel the urge to become a better person, and yet at the same time I experience the nagging certainty that I'm not likely to change very much.

It's not so different from the way I feel about the house that is my home. I know I ought to dust and hoover more often; if someone is coming to stay I make a panicky effort, usually a lick-and-a-promise, to clean the rooms. But sadly, and I admit not very sadly, I am all too aware that I will never be a model housewife.

At the end of the 1980s when the Berlin Wall was coming down and the Soviet hold over the Eastern bloc countries was crumbling, I got to know two young Hungarian women, Ildiko and Tunde. They invited my husband and me to visit Hungary and to stay with them in their homes.

First we went to Ildiko's house. Her father is a lawyer who had been considered useful by the Communist government and so had been allowed to stay in his beautiful, spacious house with its lovely gardens overlooking the city of Budapest. We were very happy with this generous, cultivated and interesting family and admired their paintings and fine furniture.

After a few days we went by train across to Debrecen to stay with Tunde and her family. This was a shock. Her parents were academics; they had been demoted under the Communist regime and their salaries were less than a child's average pocket money in England. Tunde met us at the railway station and we walked towards her home. My spirits sank when I saw where it was: high up in a grey concrete block of flats identical with the other soulless concrete blocks around. There were no trees, flowers or grassy spaces to be seen.

We approached the flat in a creaking lift and entered Tunde's home to a smiling welcome from her parents. The flat was tiny, but it was bright with colour, full of books and interesting pictures. The contrast between this warm, friendly and imaginative space and its grim surroundings was astonishing. That evening Tunde's parents shyly played a duet for us on the oboe and the bassoon.

Idiko and Tunde are both delightful. They are highly intelligent, cultured and well educated. Their knowledge of European, even English, history and literature puts us to shame. Without hesitation, Tunde will tell you the date of the Synod of Whitby, or in which of Shakespeare's plays the phrase 'rosemary for remembrance' occurs.

Their houses, seen from the outside, could not be more different, yet within each of them is a place where I believe Jesus would happily make his home, for 'where is love and loving-kindness, God is fain to dwell'.

*　　*　　*

Jesus and inequality

There was a rich man who was dressed in purple and fine linen and who feasted sumptuously every day. And at his gate lay a poor man named Lazarus, covered with sores, who longed to satisfy his hunger with what fell from the rich man's table; even the dogs would come and lick his sores.

Luke 16. 19–21

There is no doubt that Jesus tells a good story, but of all of them, this is my least favourite. Why? Because of my personal guilt and shame; because in common with most people in the Western world I have more than I need, while millions of my brothers and sisters have nothing.

What makes me particularly ashamed is the way I behaved earlier in my life when as a newly married woman I lived in India. Now I see a clear parallel between Dives and myself, Lazarus and my servant Kelu. Probably the rich man was aware of the existence of Lazarus, as he must have passed him frequently and seen his condition. I knew of the disparity between my lifestyle and Kelu's, my comparative wealth and his poverty. I knew but didn't question it. I accepted it as the norm for people in my situation.

Kelu's official job was to drive our car but he did far more than that. When our children played outside he was their companion and unobtrusive carer; he played with them and taught them. In the six years he worked for us he was unfailingly loyal, kind and devoted. I can only recall one peccadillo: I showed him my new-born son and asked, 'What do you think, Kelu?' With a big smile and doting expression he answered, 'Ah, big and fat like Madam!' I tried to accept the compliment gracefully.

We lived in a fine old company house with large airy rooms and a wide balcony. It had a big garden where tropical shrubs and fruit trees flourished, tended by two gardeners. Our en suite bedroom was air-conditioned.

Kelu lived with his wife and children tucked away out of sight round the back of our house. In fact I never actually saw his house, although it was only a few metres away from mine, but I could well imagine that it was entirely made of coconut leaves and had no windows or chimney. Kelu lived there with his wife and two children, all of them barefoot.

I think I was a reasonably good mistress. Kelu must have known that I liked him and respected him. Certainly I did not treat him as some of my white contemporaries treated their servants, as though they belonged to a different species. Yet it is only now, after all these years, that I have come to realize how blind I was to the inequality between Kelu and me, he in his hovel and me in my grand house. Late in the day, for Kelu is dead now, my eyes have been opened. In truth there was probably little I could have done to change my own or Kelu's situation; what I could have done was recognize that he was my brother.

*   *   *

Jesus and fretting

Now as they went on their way, he entered a certain village, where a woman named Martha welcomed him into her home. She had a sister named Mary, who sat at the Lord's feet and listened to what he was saying. But Martha was distracted by her many tasks; so she came to him and asked, 'Lord, do you not care that my sister has left me to do all the work by myself? Tell her then to help me.' But the Lord answered her, 'Martha, Martha, you are worried and distracted by many things; there is need of only one thing. Mary has chosen the better part, which will not be taken from her.'

Luke 10.38–42

This is arguably the only really homely story in the New Testament, and it is pleasing to think of Jesus relaxing in the house of good friends. Sometimes our imagination takes us way off the mark and we have a picture of Jesus sitting in a comfortable armchair with Mary on a footstool at his feet, looking serene, and Martha slaving over a hot stove in the kitchen, a worried frown on her flushed face. Of course we know it wasn't really like that, but I suppose we have the same right as the Old Masters to put the stamp of our time and situation on the story.

What I most like in the passage is the gentle rebuke which Jesus gives to Martha. He speaks to her with such affection and yet he gets to the heart of what is wrong. When I read the story recently I was reminded of another gentle chiding, one I received from my friend Helen.

In our house we keep a visitors' book, and when guests leave we ask them to sign it. Over the years the comments people make seem to have become more embarrassingly complimentary, praising the garden, the food, the welcome, the peacefulness . . . However firmly we say 'Please just write your name and address', people seem to feel they must say nice things. So after Helen left we looked in the book and it was quite a shock to read just this: 'I don't know why Anthea frets so about feeding folk. Besides, we come to see you both, not to be fed, and Whitby has fine fish suppers.' How refreshing, and how honest, even if my head has shrunk a little!

However, to get back to the story. Jesus is talking about priorities, and perhaps about the balance we all need to aim for in our lives. When I think of 'Marys' I think of contemplative monks and nuns, devoting their lives to silent prayer, and when I think of 'Marthas' I think of missionaries battling to help and comfort the victims of AIDS, or busy mothers coping with families and jobs. But I know that contemplatives make time for work in their lives, often hard, menial work, and missionaries and busy mothers try to make time for prayer. As for me, it is salutary to imagine what Jesus would say to me about this.

*   *   *

Jesus and empathy

Now while Jesus was at Bethany in the house of Simon the leper, a woman came to him with an alabaster jar of very costly ointment, and she poured it on his head as he sat at the table. But when the disciples saw it, they were angry and said, 'Why this waste? For this ointment could have been sold for a large sum, and the money given to the poor.' But Jesus, aware of this, said to them, 'Why do you trouble the woman? She has performed a good service for me. For you will always have the poor with you, but you will not always have me. By pouring this ointment on my body she has prepared me for burial.'

Matthew 26.6–12

When a woman poured the contents of an expensive jar of perfume over the head of Jesus, he alone of all those present empathized with her and understood her feelings and her reasons for doing such a thing. Reading about what she did, I was reminded of my daughter Pippa and her wedding.

Pippa had been living with John for 11 years when they decided to get married. Their young daughters, aged ten and eight, were delighted and naturally excited when they were told they would be bridesmaids.

I was happy about the marriage, but not about the wedding. I just couldn't understand why my normally clear-headed, sensible daughter was going in for such razzmatazz, such extravagance. For the first time in his life, poor John was taking out a loan from the bank. Of course I said nothing, or rather, I went along with all of it. I have been long enough a mother to know how golden silence is, how unproductive interference, so Pippa spent more money on the sort of things that seem frivolous to me. The wedding was to be perfect, beautiful and wonderful. So Pippa bought a stunningly lovely (and stunningly expensive) pure white dress. She had matching frocks for the bridesmaids, the exact soft green and pink of the flowers in her bouquet, and so on and so on.

I knew I should make the best of it. I also bought a new dress, and even a hat, and I smiled at everyone. Inside I still felt critical and cross, until the moment when I saw how much John loved Pippa and how much she loved him in return. All at once I understood. They were happy, and I was happy too.

*　　　*　　　*

Jesus and adultery

The scribes and the Pharisees brought a woman who had been caught in adultery; and making her stand before all of them, they said to him, 'Teacher, this woman was caught in the very act of committing adultery. Now in the law Moses commanded us to stone such women. Now what do you say?' They said this to test him, so that they might have some charge to bring against him. Jesus bent down and wrote with his finger on the ground. When they kept on questioning him, he straightened up and said to them, 'Let anyone among you who is without sin be the first to throw a stone at her.' And once again he bent down and wrote on the ground. When they heard it, they went away, one by one, beginning with the elders; and Jesus was left alone with the woman standing before him. Jesus straightened up and said to her, 'Woman, where are they? Has no one condemned you?' She said, 'No one, sir.' And Jesus said, 'Neither do I condemn you. Go your way, and from now on, do not sin again.'

John 8.3–11

I find this a particularly moving story and also a puzzling one for me. For instance, what was Jesus writing in the sand? Why did he show no disapproval, either to the men or to the woman? Why was the man responsible not mentioned? After all, it takes two to commit adultery! Jesus seems to show a curious detachment. His writing in the sand suggests he was only half-listening, half-looking. And yet we can be sure he was absorbing everything about the scene.

Recently I was at a service where the Archbishop of York, John Sentamu, was preaching. He invited people to ask him questions, and one person asked his opinion on the question of homosexuality. The archbishop paused a moment, before saying that these matters were not of central importance to him. He said that what he believes, as a Christian, is important is to love God and love one another. He was echoing the words of Jesus to one of the Pharisees:

> [Jesus] said to him, '"You shall love the Lord your God with all your heart, and with all your soul and with all your mind." This is the greatest and first commandment. And a second is like it: "You shall love your neighbour as yourself." On these two commandments hang all the law and the prophets.'
>
> Matthew 22.37–40

I think in answer to the questioner the archbishop was also echoing the attitude of Jesus to the woman in the story.

His words to the scribes and Pharisees surely pierce us to the marrow, for we too know ourselves to be sinners. And in his words to the woman we can sense his pity, his mercy and his authority.

*   *   *

Jesus the radical

> *The Pharisees and their scribes were complaining to his disciples, saying, 'Why do you eat with tax-collectors and sinners?'*
>
> Luke 5.30

Jesus always dared to be different. He did not behave as Pharisees were expected to behave. Inclusivity was much more important to him than conformity. He was a brave radical.

The most radical person I have known personally was Dr Roggendorf. Hubert Roggendorf grew up in Nazi Germany, and was the only boy in his school to refuse to join the Nazi Youth. At university he was one of only three students who dared to take the same courageous step. Forced to join the German army, he worked as a doctor tending the wounded regardless of their nationality. I came across him in a very different capacity. Working as a missionary doctor, he delivered my first and second babies.

Dr Roggendorf had decided to give up ten years of his life to work in a developing country. He took his wife and six children to south India, where they lived in poverty. Their house was quite unlike any of the spacious houses of the other Europeans in the area; so was their lifestyle. They lived in a hut with no electricity and no running water.

Jesus was radical in that he seemed unafraid to reject the conventions of his time, unafraid to befriend those whom society despised, unafraid to stand up and be counted.

Hubert Roggendorf may have been afraid when as a boy he stood up to the Nazis and refused to go along with the policies he could not condone, but afraid or not, he too stood up to be counted. In India he had a radical way of life; his close friends were Malayali, not European. He was a devout Christian who lived his life to the full and gave years of his life to save the poorest. It is a rare privilege to have known such a true follower of Christ as Hubert.

*   *   *

Jesus and slavery

And during supper Jesus, knowing that the Father had given all things into his hands, and that he had come from God and was going to God, got up from the table, took off his outer robe, and tied a towel around himself. Then he poured water into a basin and began to wash the disciples' feet and to wipe them with the towel that was tied around him. He came to Simon Peter, who

*said to him, 'Lord, are you going to wash my feet?' Jesus
answered, 'You do not know now what I am doing, but later
you will understand.' Peter said to him, 'You will never wash
my feet.' Jesus answered, 'Unless I wash you, you have no share
with me.' Simon Peter said to him, 'Lord, not my feet only but
also my hands and my head!' . . . After he had washed their feet,
had put on his robe, and had returned to the table, he said to
them, 'Do you know what I have done to you? You call me
Teacher and Lord – and you are right, for that is what I am. So
if I, your Lord and Teacher, have washed your feet, you also
ought to wash one another's feet.'*

John 13.3–9, 12–14

It seems to me that washing his disciples' feet was one of the most
powerful of the deeds of Jesus. He was making an important statement, all the more moving because it was told not in words but in
action. We can tell clearly from Peter's reaction that the disciples
were startled and in his case shocked to the core, and this must
mean that the idea of master and servant, superior and inferior,
was a deeply held conviction, which Jesus was manifestly over-
turning.

The slave trade and slave exploitation in the West Indies are
probably the most scandalous manipulation of the master–
servant relationship in the world's history. It is almost unbearable
to read how human beings were treated with such appalling
cruelty by their fellows, in Africa, on the terrible sea voyage across
the Atlantic and on the plantations of the Caribbean.

Two hundred years ago, the Quakers and other like-minded
activists, with William Wilberforce as their figurehead and
spokesman, succeeded in bringing about the abolition of the slave
trade, and 21 years later slavery in the West Indies was itself
abolished.

English people may feel some pride that their forebears were
responsible for the abolition; more thoughtful folk may feel

considerable guilt for their treatment of slaves in the first place. But neither pride nor guilt are appropriate, only an increasing understanding of why this dreadful episode was ever allowed to develop.

We might ask what our descendants, 200 years into the future, will think of us when they look back to our time. I think it likely that they will be horrified by the way we in the West treat our fellow humans in developing countries, the way we have failed to make poverty history. When I think about the slave transporters, owners and traders, I ask, 'How *could* they?'

Perhaps one day someone will ask that about me.

*   *   *

Jesus and touch

Once, when he was in one of the cities, there was a man covered with leprosy. When he saw Jesus, he bowed with his face to the ground and begged him, 'Lord, if you choose, you can make me clean.' Then Jesus stretched out his hand, touched him, and said, 'I do choose. Be made clean.' Immediately the leprosy left him.

Luke 5.12–13

When the leper felt the touch of Jesus he must have been overwhelmed by a turmoil of emotions: disbelief, amazement and, even before his miraculous healing, profound gratitude. Nobody touched lepers; nobody went near them if they could help it.

My friend David told me a true story in which a touch affected him deeply, not only physically but emotionally and spiritually as well. He had a vivid dream in which he was in a place of exceptional loveliness:

THE HEALING TOUCH

I could not bear the beauty of that place:
mountains and sea and sky, magnificent and pure,
unblemished and innocent.
And there stood I, insignificant
but soaked in sin. The guilt within me
rose like bile and would have swamped me.
Loathing myself, I longed to die then.
I fell to my knees and stayed there,
my head bowed, my heart crushed but fiercely
    thudding.
I could not move, nor cry out.
I closed my eyes against the loveliness
of mountains, sea and sky.
Time passed slowly.
I was unaware of cold, or stiffness
or the darkening light.
Then, after a long while,
I felt something:
at first a gentle touch on my shoulder,
then strong arms holding me fast,
warmth and strength flowing into me.
I did not move or turn my head,
but slowly, slowly, peace began
filling my weary body,
flooding my troubled soul.
I stood again, opening my eyes
and saw the mountains, sea and sky.
My companion had vanished,
but I felt gladness.
I opened my arms and sang.
I was free.

When David woke from his dream he did indeed feel free. He knew that he was forgiven, and healed.

*　　*　　*

Jesus – respect

When he entered Capernaum, a centurion came to him, appealing to him and saying, 'Lord, my servant is lying at home paralysed, in terrible distress.' And he said to him, 'I will come and cure him.' The centurion answered, 'Lord, I am not worthy to have you come under my roof; but only speak the word, and my servant will be healed. For I also am a man under authority, with soldiers under me; and I say to one, "Go", and he goes, and to another, "Come", and he comes, and to my slave, "Do this", and the slave does it.' When Jesus heard him, he was amazed and said to those who followed him, 'Truly I tell you, in no one in Israel have I found such faith.'

Matthew 8.5–10

I like the way Matthew describes Jesus as being amazed by the centurion. Sometimes there's a temptation to think of him as all-knowing, so that nothing and nobody will faze him, but clearly he did not expect the centurion to be a man of faith. He was not, after all, a Jew, like Jesus, but of an altogether different race and religion, so Jesus was surprised that such a man would trust him to heal his servant. He greatly respected the centurion.

In a similar way, I sometimes find myself having unconscious reservations about people who are not Christians. I know and firmly believe that God's Spirit moves where it will, that love and generosity and courage and self-sacrifice are by no means exclusively the virtues of Christians or religious people. And yet I have

37

to admit that I was surprised to learn that my young friends Peter and Sally are not Christians and are if anything somewhat suspicious of churches and organized religion. They are people I respect and admire as much as anyone I know.

When we first got to know them, Sally was a nurse working with victims of abuse and Peter a doctor working full-time with a practice for people seeking asylum and refugees. He was extremely patient, showing respect for his clients, giving them space to cry and providing an interpreter so that they could tell their stories of rape and torture. When he provided medical reports to lawyers who were dealing with such cases, he gave away all the fees he received to a local fund for helping people seeking asylum.

Those who knew Peter and Sally and the way they spent their lives were full of admiration for their dedication and generosity, but now we are even more impressed because after some years they have handed over their work to other professionals, and have gone to live in a remote part of Uganda. There they work in a missionary hospital, caring for the poorest of the poor. It is very tough, tougher than they had imagined. Living conditions are difficult but that is nothing compared to all the problems they have to face. One small example: soon after they arrived, Sally discovered her senior nurse stealing drugs. Inevitably Sally sacked her, but a few days later she was deeply distressed to be told that 17 people depended on that nurse's salary for survival.

There is no doubt that Peter and Sally are wonderful young people, deserving the greatest respect that we can give them.

*   *   *

Jesus – anger

'Woe to you, scribes and Pharisees, hypocrites! For you tithe mint, dill, and cummin, and have neglected the weightier matters of the law: justice and mercy and faith. It is these you ought to have practised without neglecting the others. You blind guides! You strain out a gnat but swallow a camel!

'Woe to you, scribes and Pharisees, hypocrites! For you clean the outside of the cup and of the plate, but inside they are full of greed and self-indulgence. You blind Pharisee! First clean the inside of the cup, so that the outside also may become clean.

'Woe to you, scribes and Pharisees, hypocrites! For you are like whitewashed tombs, which on the outside look beautiful, but inside they are full of the bones of the dead and of all kinds of filth. So you also on the outside look righteous to others, but inside you are full of hypocrisy and lawlessness.'

Matthew 23.23–28

Phew! Is this the gentle Jesus meek and mild Victorian hymn-writers described? Is it the tender, loving, compassionate Jesus we know from the Gospels? Well, yes, it's the same person. Jesus was human with all the different facets of personality that humans have. None of us is one-dimensional. Sometimes he was an angry young man.

Anger is not in itself a sin, although the way we express it can be. Obviously it is wrong to beat a child in anger, and even words can be cruel and harmful. But there is such a thing as righteous anger which it is legitimate to use when we want to speak out against injustice. In this passage Jesus is speaking, or perhaps shouting, at the scribes and Pharisees in righteous indignation.

The adjective most people would use to describe Ian is 'good-humoured'. I have also heard it said of him: 'He's a real gentleman.' I'm not quite sure what that means, but I, too, find him good-humoured, gentle, mild-mannered and altogether pleasant.

One day I was walking with him when we saw ahead of us a lad of about 15 punching a much smaller boy. By the time we reached them the little one was on the ground, crying, and the bully had started to kick him. Suddenly, Ian's voice rang out: 'Stop it, stop it at once, you coward! How dare you treat this little boy like this?' The bully was about to run, but Ian caught him by the arm and held on to him firmly. By now I had pulled the small boy to his feet and was wiping away his tears. Ian began to shout and use language of the sort I had never expected to hear from his lips. A crowd was beginning to gather and I wished I could creep away. Then, when someone in the crowd began joining in, jeering at the bully, Ian stopped suddenly. He asked the boy his name and the name of his school and let him go.

He was red in the face and grinned at me sheepishly. 'Sorry about that display,' he said. 'I just can't stand bullies! Now let's get this little fellow home.'

Afterwards, I thought over what had happened. Ian's reaction had surely been too vehement – or had it? I hoped the bully had been taught a lesson and that the little boy would not be beaten up again, but I did wonder what I would have done if I had been on my own, without Ian. I hope I would have been brave enough to show my anger.

*   *   *

Jesus – weeping

Jesus wept.

John 11.35, Jerusalem Bible

These two words are given a whole verse in the Bible, and rightly so, because they contain one of the most powerful statements in the gospel. Why is this? I think the bare statement 'Jesus wept' reveals Jesus at his most human.

He weeps spontaneously, from his gut, because his dear friend has died. It doesn't matter that his divine self knows at some level that he will have the power to raise Lazarus from the dead. It doesn't matter that the people around look up to him as Lord and Master. Jesus just weeps because he feels sorrow just as you and I do.

Jesus wept for his friend who had died. We all mourn in different ways. We grieve because someone we loved is with us no more, and we know we will miss them. This is to grieve for ourselves, but our sadness is often for the dead person too, especially if they are young. We feel that so much potential, so much happiness and fulfilment has been denied them.

Paradoxically, even those who believe that those we love are now with God feel this way; it's simply part of being human.

There are no rules about mourning. I used to work with bereaved people, and no two were alike in their behaviour, attitudes, the pattern of their grieving or the length of their time of deep sorrow. Some wept copiously, some were almost incapable of speech, others spoke without drawing breath. Some were very near despair, others could laugh from time to time. We can never judge, only be a channel of God's love.

When my baby of five months died I didn't weep. I thought, and probably I was mistaken to think like this, that I should not show how much I was grieving because it was my duty to be strong for my family. I tried to be calm and to behave normally.

It may have been partly because of this that my two youngest children, Lizzie and Pippa, didn't realize what had happened. In any case Lizzie was only five years old, and Pippa still younger; they couldn't have understood what it meant to die.

One day I came across the little girls playing with a doll. Pippa was holding it, and Lizzie said, 'No, Pip, hold him like Mummy holds Ben.' And she showed her sister how to cradle the doll in her arms.

I just ran into another room, closed the door and collapsed on the sofa in tears, floods of healing tears.

I think I should have wept sooner, because I would have been healed sooner, and *then* I would have been stronger for my children.

∗   ∗   ∗

Jesus – an all-rounder?

. . . they took him with them in the boat, just as he was. Other boats were with him. A great gale arose, and the waves beat into the boat, so that the boat was already being swamped. But he was in the stern, asleep on the cushion; and they woke him up . . .

Mark 4.36–38

Most of the great paintings of Jesus show him wearing a halo or dressed in a white garment, so that he is marked out as someone set apart and holy. This is how we tend to think of him too, but I believe he probably did not always behave as someone set apart and holy, rather as a normal man who enjoyed eating a meal or going for a walk with his friends.

We rightly associate Jesus with the word 'love', because his love, like his Father's, was all-embracing and unconditional, but I guess that he would often actually *like* people as well. The things he said and the things he did were so amazing that we forget that in his spare time he probably wanted to be like everybody else. He must have been a very good friend to those who knew him.

Mark's is by far the shortest Gospel, yet sometimes he surprises us by including details which the other evangelists omit. In his account of the stilling of the storm, he has two such additions. He tells us that the disciples took Jesus into the boat '*just as he was*'.

I find this phrase puzzling: what can it mean? I asked my husband what the phrase meant to him and he said, 'He hadn't gone home to change.' This would hardly apply to Jesus! Perhaps it means something like 'tired as he was'.

Once in the boat, Mark tells us, he fell asleep '*on a cushion*'; this is a picture no-one else includes but gives us the impression that Jesus relaxed comfortably, at home among his friends.

I once lived in community with a group of religious sisters. One of them seemed 'set apart and holy'. She spent long hours in silent prayer, and sometimes, when during community meetings someone suggested we might pray, she would close her eyes and lapse into a silence so deep and so long that the rest of us would be driven to fidgeting, coughing loudly and even giggling.

But this nun had a different side to her character. The community ran a retreat centre, and one year a group of male retreatants challenged us to a football match. We were mostly women of all shapes, sizes and ages, but we all gladly agreed.

The retreatants would have beaten us easily had it not been for Sister Rosa. She stood between the goalposts and valiantly fended off every ball that was kicked in her direction. She must have been badly bruised, but she was unquestionably 'Woman of the Match'.

*   *   *

Jesus – his Father

When I lay in that pigsty
(oh how I hated it!)
and couldn't sleep,
I would think about home.
Once it had seemed so boring,
now it seemed like paradise.

I used to wonder,
could I go back?
Mostly I thought of my father,
and wondered.
He was such a good man
always kind and patient
loving me and my brother
but I know I had hurt him cruelly,
I must have broken his heart.
I thought he might have missed me for a while,
but there was always my older brother,
a good man, unlike me,
honest and hardworking.
He would be my father's consolation,
and I would be forgotten.

I finally found the courage
to make my way home.
There was just a chance, I thought,
a slim chance, for my loving father
was also a just man,
that he would take me back
to work as his servant.

So when I came over the hill
and saw him standing at the gate
saw him start at the sight of me
and come running,
my frail, dignified old father, running!
I collapsed in astonishment.
I fell to my knees
and started to gabble something,
but he pulled me to my feet
and clasped me in his arms.

He was so happy,
full of joy to see me!
I began in that moment
to understand what love means.

The story of the Prodigal Son is so powerfully told that in reading it or listening to it we can get carried along and absorbed by the drama to such an extent that we forget that it *is* a story. It has all the ingredients of a good yarn: a villain, a hero, a sub-plot, dramatic surprise, a twist in the tail and a happy ending. But it is much more than that. It is showing us what our God is really like, and the person telling us is Jesus, the one who knows him intimately. None of the other writers in the Bible can grasp the essence of God in the way that Jesus does. And we know he is telling the story so that we, with our feebler minds and less sensitive souls, can at least come nearer to understanding the depth of that unfailing love – made up of forgiveness, tenderness and joy – which God pours out on us sinners.

*   *   *

Jesus – homelessness

As they were going along the road, someone said to him, 'I will follow you wherever you go.' And Jesus said to him, 'Foxes have their holes, and birds of the air have nests; but the Son of Man has nowhere to lay his head.'

Luke 9.57–58

We do not get a sense here that Jesus is complaining; nowhere in the Gospels does he show any sign of self-pity. Rather, he is stating a fact. Sometimes he seems to have stayed with friends or perhaps relations of his disciples; at other times, when he was travelling, he would have found some rough shelter or slept in the open.

Today, in the Western world, it is a scandal that so many people of all ages have nowhere to lay their heads, who sleep under bridges, in doorways, on park benches and railway platforms. Sometimes newspaper reporters have tried to sleep rough for a week or two, in order to bring the plight of the homeless more vividly to their readers, but like all such experiments, these efforts can never be quite authentic. You have to be genuinely homeless to understand what it is really like. Jesus did understand this; he wasn't homeless from choice or to prove a point.

I have a good friend whose working life was spent with the Salvation Army. She was posted for a number of years in Notting Hill, London, and each Christmas Ann and her colleague Dorothy gave a special festive lunch for any lonely people who lived nearby and for the local homeless. Ann told me that one Christmas the flat above the hall, where she and Dorothy lived, was being refurbished. Ann said she complained bitterly to her friend, saying, 'What sort of Christmas is this, with no wallpaper and no carpets?' The party was a great success, and a group of homeless men were particularly grateful. When it was over and these men were about to leave, one of them said, 'Won't you come and see where we live, Major?'

So the two women went with their new friends. Under the concrete walkways of the South Bank the homeless men showed Ann and Dorothy their home. Their sleeping bags were stowed along a ledge, together with a display of Christmas cards and decorations. Ann told me she felt very humbled.

I think there is a danger of forgetting not only the dignity of many homeless people, but also the warmth and strength of the friendships they form.

*   *   *

Jesus and rejection

As he was setting out on a journey, a man ran up and knelt before him, and asked him, 'Good Teacher, what must I do to inherit eternal life?' Jesus said to him, 'Why do you call me good? No one is good but God alone. You know the commandments: "You shall not murder; You shall not commit adultery; You shall not steal; You shall not bear false witness; You shall not defraud; Honour your father and mother."' He said, 'Teacher, I have kept all these since my youth.' Jesus, looking at him, loved him and said, 'You lack one thing; go, sell what you own, and give the money to the poor, and you will have treasure in heaven; then come, follow me.' When he heard this, he was shocked and went away grieving, for he had many possessions.

Mark 10.17–22

Mark tells us that the young man went away sad. It seems probable that he was not the only one to feel sad; Jesus must have been disappointed that the young man could not bring himself to give up his wealth, but I think he would also have felt unhappy at a different level: Mark says that Jesus looked steadily at the young man, and loved him, so he surely would have hoped that he would stay and become his friend. There is a sense in which both of them, in different ways, suffered rejection.

It is a natural human experience to find rejection hard to bear, and this is why I am appalled by the current tendency of television producers to engineer programmes which deliberately set out to humiliate and reject people in front of the viewing public. Personally, I find such programmes too painful to watch, but I do know that their appeal lies in the spectacle of people suffering rejection while millions of viewers watch, much as the Romans enjoyed seeing gladiators fight centuries ago, or as eager mobs crowded in front of the gallows to see a wretched miscreant hang in more recent times.

Of course it isn't the same: nobody is getting killed or hurt, at least not physically, and a lot of people must consider it harmless fun or the programme makers would not continue to make such shows. But I find it sad that it is thought necessary to pander to, and indeed encourage, the instinct of one human being to take pleasure in the humiliation of another.

Recently I did, by chance, switch on my television at the end of one of these programmes. Various people had been competing, hoping to be chosen to represent Britain in the Eurovision Song Contest. When I switched on, only two 'acts' had survived as far as the final: a lively group of four and a solo girl singer. As, with much razzmatazz, the winner was to be declared, the camera zoomed in on the tense face of the young woman, and when it was her name that was announced, the tension vanished and her face lit up with joy. Then, only seconds later, someone announced that there had been a mistake. The girl singer had lost and now counted for nothing.

We could argue that this was a salutary experience. We could point out that this young woman had presumably entered the competition of her own free will. But whatever the circumstances, public rejection is painful and humiliating.

*   *   *

Jesus and creation

It is my favourite time of year: the end of April and the beginning of May. This morning the sky was cloudless and the sun very warm. We went out into the countryside where we saw tiny new-born lambs and listened to the birds singing. The hedges were just greening; half the trees were still bare and half in new leaf. Primroses and violets were growing along the banks of the river and in the clear light the flanks of the hillside glowed purple and green and bronze. Here and there in the landscape fields of oilseed rape made a vivid splash of yellow.

As I drank in all this loveliness I was thinking about Jesus and wondering about his attitude, as a human being, to the creation he, as God, had brought into being. Was he so absorbed in his exhausting ministry of healing and teaching that he simply didn't have time to notice the wonders of nature, to stand and stare? Then I remembered what he said to his disciples when he was telling them not to worry about their lives, about what they had to eat or to wear:

> Consider the lilies, how they grow: they neither toil nor spin, yet I tell you, even Solomon in all his glory was not clothed like one of these.
>
> Luke 12.27

The lilies, that is the wild flowers of Galilee, spring into bloom at this time of year. I have only seen them in photographs, but they are a glorious riot of every colour, not unlike the wild flowers that grow in Britain in fields that have not been sprayed with weed-killer, though the Galilean flowers are more exuberant.

Jesus must have rejoiced in the annual appearance of these beautiful flowers, and it is interesting that in his eyes they were even more glorious than the royal robes of Solomon. I take this as a small sign, but a sure sign, of his appreciation of the wonder of creation.

*　　　*　　　*

Jesus and crowds

Jesus departed with his disciples to the lake, and a great multi-
tude from Galilee followed him; hearing all that he was doing,
they came to him in great numbers from Judea, Jerusalem,
Idumea, beyond the Jordan, and the region around Tyre and
Sidon. He told his disciples to have a boat ready for him because
of the crowd, so that they would not crush him; for he had
cured many, so that all who had diseases pressed upon him to
touch him.

Mark 3.7–10

I often wonder how Jesus felt about the crowds that followed him
everywhere. Was he sometimes exhausted, sometimes exasperat-
ed? I see myself as a victim of crowds because I live in a town
which is interesting, historic, in parts beautiful, a place where I am
happy and at peace, but every weekend, even in winter nowadays,
we are swamped by a tide of thousands of visitors who pollute our
air with their cars and litter our streets with the left-overs of their
fish and chips. At the height of the season it is literally a struggle
to walk down the street nearest my home, so great is the press of
noisy, sweaty humanity.

I feel cross and frustrated; only when I hear a remark like 'Isn't
it beautiful?' or 'What wouldn't I give to live here?' do I remember
how blessed I am that this is my home, how willing I should be to
share it with people who come, perhaps for just half a day, and,
even seeing it at its worst, are delighted to be here.

When I was a young student, I used to go to the Lake District
every year with a group of friends, walking the hills and conquer-
ing quite a few summits. Circumstances meant that after university I didn't go back to the Lakes for about ten years, and I hadn't
realized that year by year more and more tourists had made those
hills and valleys more commercialized and less tranquil.

I was very excited to be taking our four young children to visit this place I had talked about so much. We took a cottage belonging to friends for a week, and arrived late on Saturday. On Sunday we set off for our first walk. It rained heavily all day and we couldn't see beyond a couple of feet ahead of us because of the constant downpour; very soon I felt the rain trickling through and beneath my underwear. I have never been so wet in my life and our children were hardly amused.

However, Monday dawned bright and fair, and I decided this would be the high point of our week: my young sons and daughters would scale the highest peak in England! Well, they did, in company with at least a thousand other people. I had forgotten it was a Bank Holiday. A long, long line of us queued up to the summit, literally treading in the footsteps of the person in front. For me it was a crushing disappointment.

Perhaps Jesus had similar experiences and even, at times, similar feelings, because we know that big crowds followed him everywhere. We also know that he sometimes escaped and went off on his own to pray. Once, at least, he tried to get away with his disciples who needed a break and a rest. But when the crowds guessed where he was going they followed him and caught up with him. Then he took pity on them because he knew their need. I know I should consider the needs of the people who come to my town. And it is salutary to admit that I have several times been very happy myself to be part of a big crowd: when I 'marched', or rather strolled, through the streets of Glasgow in solidarity with those opposed to the war in Iraq, or joined with all the thousands who met in Edinburgh to proclaim that we must make poverty history. Those were great occasions for me, but not quite as moving as the time when we went to Taizé and half-knelt, half-sat in the smallest possible space among a thousand or so other bodies in the total silence of worship.

I'm afraid the difference between Jesus and me is that whereas I quite often come near to hating the crowds, Jesus never failed to love them.

*   *   *

Jesus and mountains

And after he had dismissed the crowds, he went up the mountain by himself to pray.

Matthew 14.23

Six days later, Jesus took with him Peter and James and John, and led them up a high mountain apart, by themselves.

Mark 9.2

For me it is easy to understand why Jesus chose to go up into the hills to pray, because I find that a solitary place in the mountains is the best place for being still before God. Even the most noble arches of cathedrals don't lift my heart and mind to worship in the way that mountains do. What is most moving about such an experience is the way I am aware simultaneously of the awesomeness of our great God and of his infinite tenderness towards humankind.

After walking in the Cheviots in Northumberland, I tried to express this in the following lines:

> I seek you, and I find you
> all the time and everywhere:
> in chapels and churches,
> in people and places,
> in music and laughter and tears.
>
> But here, in this place,
> you come to me unbidden.
> Here, deep in the soaring hills,
> in silence and stillness and solitude,
> I know your presence,
> and in a moment of awed humility,
> I feel your touch.

*　　　*　　　*

Jesus and women

There are many remarkable things about Jesus, and one of the most striking is sometimes overlooked: his attitude to women.

When we read about the way he treated the 'bent-over' woman, the woman with a haemorrhage, the woman caught committing adultery, the Samaritan woman, to name only a few, we, especially the women among us, might feel a sense of envy or of longing, wishing we could personally encounter someone who would show us such tenderness, compassion and understanding.

Yet we have only to reflect for a moment to realize that these qualities of Jesus, his gentle affection, his pity and his empathy, are indeed ours to receive. Even today, in our secular corrupt and indifferent world, we can still turn to Jesus for consolation, forgiveness and encouragement.

In the time of Jesus, women were very largely ignored. This is not particularly evident in the Gospels, where women were often the focus of Christ's interest, although in Matthew's Gospel there is an interesting phrase, well translated in the Jerusalem Bible, 'Now four thousand men had eaten, *to say nothing of the women and children*' (Matthew 15.38). Other translations have '*not counting women and children*'. Clearly it is not necessary to mention women; they don't count.

So it must have taken considerable courage for Jesus to 'buck this trend', not only to notice women, not only to respect them, but to treat them with care and compassion, to go out of his way to heal them.

Take the case of the 'bent-over' woman. As soon as Jesus catches sight of her, he goes over and heals her, knowing he will enrage the synagogue officials for doing such a thing on the Sabbath. They make a fuss about this, but they must have been even more put out by the fact that she is only a useless old woman. Jesus, however, doesn't look at her like that; he addresses her as a 'daughter of Abraham', a title which must have astonished and delighted her and restored her dignity.

Now he was teaching in one of the synagogues on the sabbath. And just then there appeared a woman with a spirit that had crippled her for eighteen years. She was bent over and was quite unable to stand up straight. When Jesus saw her, he called her over and said, 'Woman, you are set free from your ailment.' When he laid his hands on her, immediately she stood up straight and began praising God. But the leader of the synagogue, indignant because Jesus had cured on the sabbath, kept saying to the crowd, 'There are six days on which work ought to be done; come on those days and be cured, and not on the sabbath day.' But the Lord answered him and said, 'You hypocrites! Does not each of you on the sabbath untie his ox or his donkey from the manger, and lead it away to give it water? And ought not this woman, a daughter of Abraham whom Satan bound for eighteen long years, be set free from this bondage on the sabbath day?' When he said this, all his opponents were put to shame; and the entire crowd was rejoicing at all the wonderful things that he was doing.

Luke 13.10–17

THE BENT-OVER WOMAN

I had been like this for more than half my life,
eighteen long years,
years of pain and misery and despair.
It didn't take long for Matthat to throw me out.
I understood. Nobody wants a cripple for a wife.
I had hopes of Joda, my first-born,
the apple of my eye. He was fifteen when it happened.
I thought he might come and see me sometimes,
bring me food, even money.
But he never came. I have been so hungry.

I couldn't understand why I was still alive.
I wished I wasn't. There was nothing for me in life.
I was bent so low I could see nothing,
only my feet and a bit of ground.
I wandered about, begging, and sometimes, in
    desperation, stealing,
though that wasn't easy in my condition.
Children jeered at me. Some threw sticks and stones,
a grown man raised a whip to me
and told me to get out of his sight.
I knew I was nothing, but sometimes
I wondered about God, wondered if I counted as
    nothing to him.
And one day I made my way to the synagogue.
I stood outside near the door. I could hear men praying.
I crept inside a little, and suddenly
I heard a voice, saying, 'Woman you are free from your
    ailment.'
At first, I didn't think this was anything to do with me,
but I felt strong hands on my shoulders and yes!
slowly I straightened. I was healed, and now I could
    see him,
the man Jesus. Oh, how I praised God!
But the best was yet to come.
The official was angry with Jesus
because he had cured me on the Sabbath,
but he answered them and called me
a 'daughter of Abraham'! I stood straight then.
I stood tall. I wasn't nothing any more.

Another encounter which shows Jesus' unusual attitude towards
women, and indeed to the prevailing way of thinking about them
in his day, is the story of the woman who was caught in the act of
adultery which has already been touched on in this book. It is sad

that two thousand years after John's account of this happening, there are still countries in the world where women are punished by death for adultery while men guilty of the same sin get off scot-free.

The way Jesus dealt with the situation must have been a salutary lesson for the scribes and Pharisees. The rather sudden self-knowledge of the doctors of the law, beginning with the eldest, is particularly moving.

We can imagine the poor woman's fear and shame as she stood in front of Jesus with all those 'good and holy' men behind her. And we can imagine her incredulity as the men walked away, her huge sense of relief followed by gratitude such as she had never known. Jesus had given her a life-changing experience.

THE GUILTY WOMAN

I was terrified, shaking all over.
I thought the worst had happened
when Melchi found us together, Jannai and me.
I thought he would shout and fetch a whip to flog me.
I could have borne that.
But he just stood there, staring, white-faced, his eyes
    bulging,
then he went out. I knew that wasn't the end of it.
Jannai ran, without even a word to me or a look.
I waited, and sure enough it wasn't long
before Melchi came back, and with him his friends,
the good and holy men, Pharisees and scribes.
They dragged me down to the temple.
I couldn't stop shaking.
They stood me in front of the man Jesus,
and told him what I had done.
Standing there in my shame,
I might as well have been naked.

I waited for him to condemn me.
I knew I was going to die.
I prayed that the first stone would kill me.
But Jesus didn't even look at me, or at them.
He was on his knees, writing something in the sand.
And when they kept questioning him,
egging him on to say I should be stoned to death,
he said nothing. At last he spoke,
and I couldn't believe what I was hearing.
He said, gravely, 'If there is anyone among you that has
    not sinned,
let him be the first to throw a stone at her.'
I stood quite still, holding my breath, and waited,
wondering which part of my body the first stone
    would hit.
But one by one my accusers walked away.
When they had gone, Jesus looked up.
I was no longer afraid, but deeply ashamed.
'Woman, where are they?' he said,
'Has no one condemned you?'
'No one, sir,' I said, my voice trembling.
'Neither do I condemn you,' he said.
'Go on your way, and from now on, don't sin again.'
I felt cleansed, and free, and at peace.

Now I would like to look at another account of a meeting between
Jesus and a woman, this one arguably the most extraordinary of
all such encounters.

But he [Jesus] had to go through Samaria. So he came to a
Samaritan city called Sychar, near the plot of ground that
Jacob had given to his son Joseph. Jacob's well was there, and
Jesus, tired out by his journey, was sitting by the well. It was
about noon.

A Samaritan woman came to draw water, and Jesus said to her, 'Give me a drink.' (His disciples had gone to the city to buy food.) The Samaritan woman said to him, 'How is it that you, a Jew, ask a drink of me, a woman of Samaria?' (Jews do not share things in common with Samaritans.) . . . Just then his disciples came. They were astonished that he was speaking with a woman, but no one said, 'What do you want?' or, 'Why are you speaking with her?' Then the woman left her water-jar and went back to the city. She said to the people, 'Come and see a man who told me everything I have ever done! He cannot be the Messiah, can he?' They left the city and were on their way to him.

John 4.4–9, 27–30

Here Jesus is cutting right across convention. He is talking to a woman, surprising (and to some horrifying) enough, but the woman is a Samaritan. Jews didn't associate with Samaritans, just as today some white people don't associate with black people if they can help it.

When his disciples find him, they are dismayed. John, in his Gospel, uses the Greek word *ethaumazon*, meaning 'thunderstruck'. We are told that none of them asked 'What do you want?' or 'Why are you talking to her?' The implication is that these are the questions they wanted to ask, but didn't dare. And the assumption is that Jesus would only be talking to a woman if he wanted something from her.

In addition to his 12 disciples, many others followed Jesus as he travelled around Galilee and Judea. Some stayed for a long time; others, like the man speaking here, would not have known him very well.

Sometimes I despair of him, I really do.
There was I, thinking he's the best bloke I've met in a
    long while.

There's no side to him, you see. He's straight as a die
and not scared of anyone. He knows how to make
    a man
feel good about himself, and he's always helping folk,
healing them even.

But then, today, I was with some of the men,
the ones who go with him everywhere,
his inner circle you might say.
We got split up from him somehow,
so we went looking, and when we found him,
well, I have to say it: I was disgusted.
I would never have thought it of him,
but there he was, in broad daylight,
chatting to a Samaritan,
And, true as I'm standing here, a woman!
I was upset, I can tell you. I mean, it's not on, is it?
And I wasn't alone. I could see that Simon
was not a happy man.

I thought I would never get over it,
But then, as we got near to him,
I saw his face.
I saw he was looking at the woman
as if she was someone important.

And I thought: that's how he looks at me
when I'm telling him stuff. I don't understand it,
I don't understand him, that's for sure.
It shook me up, seeing him there, with her,
but I know I'll just have to accept
that he's different from us,
definitely different from me,
and I reckon I'll still tag along sometimes.
He's all right, is Jesus.

Of course this is a caricature, but aren't there still people around with attitudes like this man's? And we might consider the attitude of Christ's Church towards women through the generations. There have been several outstanding Christian women in history: Teresa of Avila, Mother Teresa of Calcutta, Hildegard of Bingen, to mention just three; but when we look at church life today, especially in the Roman Catholic Church, which has no women priests, we find the role of women is mainly to clean the church, do the flowers, make tea and coffee and bake cakes for bunfights and bazaars. And yet, when a Quiet Day or a retreat is arranged for a parish or a diocese, far and away the majority of those interested enough to attend are, in my experience, women.

So we still have a lot to question and to learn.

*   *   *

Jesus speaking of himself

When we are looking at Scripture to try and discern what Jesus was like, it may be helpful to look at the things he says about himself. John has recorded several instances where Jesus describes himself in a powerful image. According to John, Jesus said: 'I am the bread of life', 'I am the light of the world', 'I am the good shepherd', 'I am the true vine'.

I think it is worth looking at each of these statements to try to understand what Jesus meant, how he saw his ministry, and perhaps something about the way he saw himself. Jesus was not boasting; he was explaining his role and the way he wanted us to respond to him and to his Father.

I am the bread of life

I am the bread of life. Your ancestors ate the manna in the wilderness, and they died. This is the bread that comes from heaven, so that one may eat of it and not die. I am the living bread that came down from heaven. Whoever eats of this bread will live for ever; and the bread that I will give for the life of the world is my flesh.

John 6.48–51

In Jesus' day, bread was the staple food, the symbol of food of any kind, used much as we do when we say 'A man must earn his bread.' In some countries, the staple is rice or pasta, or grain or potatoes. It is that without which we cannot live. So Jesus is saying that unless we have his Spirit within us our lives will be empty and fruitless. The Spirit of Jesus gives us life so that we can grow and change and be effective in the world. Just as we need food to keep our bodies alive, so we need him to enliven our souls.

Life is given whenever the Holy Spirit wills, and it is important to remember that it is not exclusively Christians who live the abundant life of the Spirit, while many of us who do call ourselves Christians sometimes deny ourselves the nourishment we need to sustain our souls.

Before Jesus ascended into heaven, he gave Peter the task of 'feeding his sheep'. He was giving Peter the care of souls, but when we think of 'bread' and 'hunger', we remember that for Jesus the care of bodies was also of paramount importance.

> Jesus is the staff of life.
> When I go to the Eucharist,
> I receive the bread,
> I receive his body.
> I am thankful.

Then I go in search of my brother,
my hungry brother in Africa.
He is crying, he is starving,
he will die soon.
I want to share my bread with him,
I want him to receive the staff of life,
but I cannot reach him,
I cannot bring him blessing.
The world's powerful block my way.

One day I find my sister
in a shanty town in Chile.
She invites me to share her bread.
I go to her home
and find her weeping.
There is no bread to give me.
But her neighbour comes softly
and gives her half of a stale loaf of bread.
She breaks it and shares it with me.
We give thanks together
and laugh for sheer joy.
It is a Eucharist.

Jesus knows our need.

I am the light of the world

Again Jesus spoke to them, saying, 'I am the light of the
world. Whoever follows me will never walk in darkness but
will have the light of life.'

John 8.12

It seems to me that nothing is as beautiful as light. It dispels darkness, it enhances the loveliness of hills and rivers and the sea, it brings life to trees and flowers and all things that grow. It falls softly at dawn and at dusk; it shines in the eyes of children. Light, like Jesus, is beneficial, a blessing to all humankind.

Jesus was always the light of the world, right from his conception. In the book of the prophet Isaiah, we read:

The people who walked in darkness have seen a great light; those who lived in a land of deep darkness – on them light has shined . . . For a child has been born for us, a son given to us; authority rests upon his shoulders; and he is named Wonderful Counsellor, Mighty God, Everlasting Father, Prince of Peace.

Isaiah 9.2, 6

Suppose electricity
failed over the whole world.
Imagine the stars dimmed
and the smooth, shining disc of the moon
eclipsed for ever.
What if the sun
that flushes the sky with glory
never rose again,
the little leaves on the silver birch
lost their November gold
and every candle flame
flickered for the last time
and died . . . ?

Even then,
we would not live in darkness,
because, in the moment of Incarnation,
a great light shone,
a child was born,
and God became human.

Jesus blesses us, but he also challenges.

> You are the light of the world. A city built on a hill cannot be hidden. No one after lighting a lamp puts it under the bushel basket, but on the lampstand, and it gives light to all in the house. In the same way, let your light shine before others, so that they may see your good works and give glory to your Father in heaven.
>
> Matthew 5.14–16

I find this challenge frightening. I am very conscious of my weakness and failings, so how can I be any sort of light to other people? I remember as a small child singing:

> Jesus bids us shine
> With a pure, clear light,
> Like a little candle
> Burning in the night.

but even at the age of five or six I doubt if I could be a pure, clear light to anyone! And now when I have been and still am guilty of selfishness, and a host of other sins, how could I possibly be a light to anyone? The answer is that however weak and sinful I may be, still the light of Christ can shine through me. Even I can be a channel of his light and love.

I am the good shepherd

> I am the good shepherd.
>
> John 10.11

There are many references to shepherds, bad ones as well as good, in the Old Testament. One of the best-known and best-loved hymns is taken from Psalm 23.1–4:

The LORD is my shepherd, I shall not want.
He makes me lie down in green pastures;
he leads me beside still waters;
he restores my soul.
He leads me in right paths
for his name's sake.

Even though I walk through the darkest valley,
I fear no evil;
for you are with me;
your rod and your staff –
they comfort me.

In this psalm attributed to David, who was of course himself a shepherd boy, the shepherd is seen as an image of God who takes care of his people in all circumstances. Isaiah takes up the same idea of God, who, though he comes with power, maintaining his authority,

... will feed his flock like a shepherd;
he will gather the lambs in his arms,
and carry them in his bosom,
and gently lead the mother sheep.

Isaiah 40.11

This picture reveals the tenderness of God, and Ezekiel continues in this vein.

I myself will be the shepherd of my sheep, and I will make them lie down, says the Lord GOD. I will seek the lost, and I will bring back the strayed, and I will bind up the injured and I will strengthen the weak ...

Ezekiel 34.15–16

Ezekiel's shepherd is equally tender, but perhaps more proactive!

Then we come to Jesus in the New Testament. He has a rather different take on the image:

> I am the good shepherd. I know my own and my own know me, just as the Father knows me and I know the Father. And I lay down my life for the sheep. I have other sheep that do not belong to this fold. I must bring them also, and they will listen to my voice.
>
> John 10.14–16

This shepherd not only cares deeply and well for his sheep, but he is willing to lay down his life for them; there is no limit to his love. And there is something different here in the reference to the other sheep not of this fold. We can only conjecture about this: Jesus could be referring to Gentiles or people of other faiths. In any case he is revealing to the Pharisees his inclusive attitude, an attitude Christians do well to take note of today. Jesus is not the shepherd of Roman Catholics, or Jews or Quakers or Hindus, he is the shepherd of all of us and it was for all of us that he laid down his life.

What about us? In what way and how far can we be shepherds in response to the example of Jesus? I think that all priests and ministers and Christian teachers should endeavour to be pastors to those in their care. A friend of mine who teaches French and is Head of Year (which means responsible for the pastoral care of pupils in that year) told me that she doesn't lie awake at night worrying about French irregular verbs, but does have sleepless nights trying to figure out ways to help children with anorexia, children who have been abused, children whose parents are addicted to drugs or drink or both, and so on. True pastoral care is hard work and emotionally draining.

Another friend, Wendy, told me about her vicar. Wendy is a widow with a young daughter of 14, Mary. For years Wendy and Mary were inseparable, doing everything together, going everywhere together. Then, from the age of about ten, Mary gradually became more and more independent, preferring to spend her time and enjoy life with friends of her own age. Wendy felt a little sad about this but realized it was quite natural and that Mary would have more fun with her chosen friends.

One thing that made Wendy happy was that Mary was evidently content to accompany her to church every Sunday. She always listened to the sermons and often talked about them with her mother afterwards, and she enjoyed singing hymns. Then abruptly, just before her fourteenth birthday, Mary announced that she didn't want to go to church any more.

'I'm sorry, Mum,' she said, 'but it's so boring.'

Only a few weeks later, the vicar left and in due course a new one was appointed. One day when Wendy was with Mary in the town, they happened to meet the new priest. He greeted Wendy with a smile, and turning to Mary, said, 'Hello, I'm Tim. You must be Wendy's daughter but I don't know your name.'

Mary responded to his friendliness and Wendy proudly told Tim that she would be taking her Grade 5 flute examination in a few days' time. One week later Mary was in town on her way home from school when she saw Tim again, walking towards her. He smiled at her warmly. 'Hi, Mary, how did the Grade 5 go?'

'He remembered my name, Mum,' Mary said later, 'and he even remembered about the exam!'

The following Sunday, Wendy tiptoed downstairs so as not to wake Mary, and so was surprised to find her already dressed.

'I thought I'd come to church, Mum, if you don't mind,' she said.

Little things like remembering people's names and what their concerns are can make a lot of difference to the people in our care.

I am the true vine

Abide in me as I abide in you. Just as the branch cannot bear fruit by itself unless it abides in the vine, neither can you unless you abide in me. I am the vine, you are the branches. Those who abide in me and I in them bear much fruit, because apart from me you can do nothing.

John 15.4–5

What is the difference between a vine and an apple tree? Clearly there are plenty of differences, but they have one thing in common: they bear fruit.

Yet there is more to a vine than this. A particularly favourite image of mine is from the first book of Kings. The narrator, writing of Solomon, says: 'During Solomon's lifetime Judah and Israel lived in safety, from Dan even to Beer-sheba, all of them under their *vines and fig trees.*' (1 Kings 4.25).

I like to imagine two old friends sitting outside, contented in the sunshine but enjoying the shade of the vine and the fig tree. And personally I would prefer to sit in the shade of an old apple tree!

We once rented a cottage in Burgundy, in a small village very near Gevrey-Chambertin which is famous throughout the world for the quality of its wine. There we got to know a delightful old man with bright eyes in a brown wrinkled face. One day, with a finger to his lips he led us into his garden, and in a quiet spot bent down and lifted the lid of what turned out to be his *petit cave*, his secret cellar, stocked with his wine which was made from his own grapes. Graciously, he poured us glasses of the wine and gave us a bottle to take home. I am no connoisseur of wine, but it did taste very good.

But this is an absurd digression. Jesus chose the vine because of the importance of its fruitfulness and the importance of being pruned. My husband, Chris, is a skilled gardener, and one year when we were looking after his sister's house while she was away on holiday, he gave her beloved and beautiful climbing rose a very thorough pruning. When Catherine came back she was aghast. 'What have you done to my poor rose?' she asked. But the following summer it bloomed as it had never bloomed before.

I think that those of us who live in the affluent parts of the world are in serious need of pruning. There is excess everywhere: too much money, too much food, too much choice, too much unquestioning self-satisfaction, too much greed. We need to get down to the bare bones of what it means to be human, and as the slogan has it, 'to live simply so that others may simply live'. We know that Jesus sometimes enjoyed the material things of life, and so should we, but in moderation.

Fruitfulness was very important to Jesus. It means not just accepting but embracing our talents, the gifts God has given us to use. It means taking on whatever task lies ahead of us and doing it as well as we can, with gratitude and joy. It might be playing the cello; it might be washing up. It also means being generous and open-hearted, for when the vine (or the apple tree) is laden with fruit, there is plenty to share and give away.

Jesus said he is the vine and we are the branches. As long as we stay grafted on to him, remaining in him and he in us, we will be safe from evil and fruitful for him.

*   *   *

The last judgement

When the Son of Man comes in his glory, and all the angels with him, then he will sit on the throne of his glory. All the nations will be gathered before him, and he will separate people one from another as a shepherd separates the sheep from the goats, and he will put the sheep at his right hand and the goats at the left. Then the king will say to those at his right hand, 'Come, you that are blessed by my Father, inherit the kingdom prepared for you from the foundation of the world; for I was hungry and you gave me food, I was thirsty and you gave me something to drink, I was a stranger and you welcomed me, I was naked and you gave me clothing, I was sick and you took care of me, I was in prison and you visited me.' Then the righteous will answer him, 'Lord, when was it that we saw you hungry and gave you food, or thirsty and gave you something to drink? And when was it that we saw you a stranger and welcomed you, or naked and gave you clothing? And when was it that we saw you sick or in prison and visited you?' And the king will answer them, 'Truly I tell you, just as you did it to one of the least of these who are members of my family, you did it to me.'

Matthew 25.31–40

Here Jesus is describing to his disciples the kind of life God wants them to lead, the kind of conduct on which they will ultimately be judged. If we apply his criteria to ourselves some of us may be surprised that our religious behaviour is not even mentioned. Jesus knows that God will not judge us on how many prayers we have said or how often we go to church, but on how we treat one another. Relationship with our brothers and sisters is what matters, and in the end it comes down to justice.

We are reminded of what Isaiah writes:

> Is such the fast that I choose,
> a day to humble oneself?
> Is it to bow down the head like a bulrush,
> and to lie in sackcloth and ashes?
> Will you call this a fast,
> a day acceptable to the LORD?

Is not this the fast that I choose:
to loose the bonds of injustice,
to undo the thongs of the yoke,
to let the oppressed go free,
and to break every yoke?
Is it not to share your bread with the hungry,
and bring the homeless poor into your house;
when you see the naked, to cover them,
and not to hide yourself from your own kin?
Then your light shall break forth like the dawn,
and your healing shall spring up quickly;
your vindicator shall go before you,
the glory of the LORD shall be your rearguard.
Then you shall call, and the LORD will answer;
you shall cry for help, and he will say, Here I am.

If you remove the yoke from among you,
the pointing of the finger, the speaking of evil,
if you offer food to the hungry
 and satisfy the needs of the afflicted,
then your light shall rise in the darkness
and your gloom be like the noonday.
The LORD will guide you continually,
and satisfy your needs in parched places,
and make your bones strong;
and you shall be like a watered garden,
like a spring of water,
whose waters never fail.

Isaiah 58.5–11

The prophet Amos goes even further:

I hate, I despise your festivals,
and I take no delight in your solemn assemblies.

Even though you offer me your burnt-offerings and
    grain-offerings,
I will not accept them;
and the offerings of well-being of your fatted animals
I will not look upon.
Take away from me the noise of your songs;
I will not listen to the melody of your harps.
But let justice roll down like waters,
and righteousness like an ever-flowing stream.

Amos 5.21–24

Jesus is clear that what God asks of his people is justice.

It is worth looking in some depth at what a commitment to a life based on justice entails.

I was hungry and you gave me food

As I write this, I am planning to take my friend to a pleasant restaurant for a meal to celebrate her fiftieth birthday. She is a very dear friend and I want to surprise her, but already I am beginning to feel guilty. I know the food will cost five or ten times more than a meal I could cook for her myself (and although I am not a very good housewife I do know how to cook!). Inevitably I think of the people in our world who have not enough to eat, and in some cases nothing. I remember that I have vowed 'to live simply so that others may simply live', the powerful slogan of justice movements.

And yet St Luke tells us that Matthew held 'a great reception' in his house in honour of Jesus, where he joined in the feasting, and the Pharisees and their scribes accused Jesus of being 'a glutton and a drunkard', saying 'John's disciples are always fasting and saying prayers, and the disciples of the Pharisees too, but yours go on eating and drinking'.

We can be sure that Jesus was not a glutton or a drunkard, but we must acknowledge that he did sometimes enjoy the pleasure of food and drink. Perhaps 'moderation in all things' is an appropriate motto for us, but always provided that we keep our awareness of the plight of the hungry at the forefront of our thinking. And, of course, awareness is not enough if we don't take any action to change the unfair distribution of wealth, and food in particular, in the countries of the world.

I was thirsty and you gave me drink

What I have said about food applies equally to drink, although the need for water among the world's poorest people is even more urgent than their need for food. Bread is the staff of life – it helps us to keep going; but water is the very *stuff* of life – without it we die.

In the Western world we grumble when there is a hosepipe ban and we can no longer water our gardens (except with a watering can) or, in the case of the rich, fill our swimming pools. At the same time in parts of the developing world, crops are failing and people are dying for lack of water.

> . . . They shall not hunger or thirst,
> neither scorching wind nor sun shall strike them down,
> for he who has pity on them will lead them,
> and by springs of water will guide them.
>
> Isaiah 49.10

But the men, women and children who are desperate for water cannot wait for the day of salvation.

Not long ago, I went walking in the hills, as I often do, with a friend. After only half an hour, I suddenly felt extremely weak. I could go no further and I longed for someone to transport me home and to bed. My companion handed me his water bottle and

I took three or four swallows. Within minutes I felt fine and we continued our walk, completing the next ten miles without mishap.

Dehydration can be dangerous, and this trivial incident reminded me of our good friend Jack who was driving in the Outback when his car broke down. He set out to try to get help, but he was carrying no water. When the search party found him it was too late. Jack had died of thirst.

When Jesus was in the depths of his anguish, he didn't cry out: 'I hurt', or 'I suffer', or 'I am forsaken'. He cried: 'I thirst.'

It is up to us to be actively concerned for those who lack water in developing countries, and also to take steps to help those who thirst for knowledge, for friendship, for love and, indeed, for God.

I was a stranger and you made me welcome

I was a stranger once. I had been living in Kerala, south India, for less than a month, when my husband and I were invited to a party to celebrate a Muslim wedding. It was a party, so I wore my party dress. It was very beautiful, the colour of flame, cut low with a full skirt. I wore my high heels too.

When we arrived at the house, the smiling host immediately took my husband away. I was left standing for a few seconds, then a small figure emerged and walked towards me smiling warmly. She was dressed in black from head to foot; only her sweet face was visible. She led me into a room where I saw with dismay that there were about a dozen more women identically dressed, all in black, and sitting cross-legged against the walls of the small room.

I was extremely embarrassed. I didn't know a word of Malayali, the local language; none of the women knew any English. 'Sticking out like a sore thumb' would be a gross understatement of the way I felt. I was of average height and weight for an Englishwoman, but I felt enormous compared to my delicate companions. I also felt that I might as well have been naked, with my bare shoulders and arms.

The smiling women made a space for me on the floor, but alas, I have always found it difficult to sit cross-legged, and manoeuvring myself into position realized that I was not only large and unseemly in my dress but also awkward and clumsy!

We sat for about an hour and we all kept smiling. The women were too polite to talk among themselves but not too polite to focus their gaze on me. At first it felt like a form of torture, but gradually I began to relax as I understood that there was no hostile or critical atmosphere in the room. On the contrary, there was warmth and welcome, mingled no doubt with astonishment.

The long silence was interrupted by the arrival of a servant, who walked round the circle placing a large leaf on everyone's lap. I was puzzled; I wondered if there was going to be some kind of ceremony. But then the boy came in again, this time carrying a large metal container and a ladle. He placed a large dollop of what I later discovered to be mutton biriyani on each leaf. It smelt wonderful, and I was eagerly waiting for some cutlery so that I could begin to eat.

But the boy didn't appear again, and the women, who were probably waiting politely for me to start, began eating – to my horror, with their fingers. Of course, I followed suit, and of course my fingers were very clumsy. I spilt the delicious biriyani on my beautiful flame-coloured dress, and watched with admiration as all the others ate with such delicacy and without spilling a drop.

It was a huge relief when the signal came for me to leave, but I took with me a sense of gratitude for the kindness and affection I had received.

Kindness and affection? Sadly, such qualities are rarely felt by the strangers who come to our country seeking asylum. Some of the press are responsible for encouraging hostility and even hatred towards strangers, giving false information about the loss of homes and jobs which are said to be the result of the arrival of refugees and people seeking asylum. In fact, asylum seekers who have been granted permission to stay in Britain, and are unable to find work, are forced to exist on a pitiful handout and are often provided with inadequate housing in which no one else is prepared to live. In fact, those whom the government decides to deport sometimes go into hiding because they know that if they return to their own country they will be tortured or killed. They receive nothing: no money, no food, no housing. They are dependent on the kindness of others to give them shelter and food. Such people have become known as 'living ghosts'.

In the Scripture the people were repeatedly exhorted to show kindness to strangers.

> When an alien resides with you in your land, you shall not oppress the alien. The alien who resides with you shall be to you as the citizen among you; you shall love the alien as yourself, for you were aliens in the land of Egypt: I am the LORD your God.
>
> Leviticus 19.33–34

> The LORD sets the prisoners free;
> the LORD opens the eyes of the blind.
> The LORD lifts up those who are bowed down;
> the LORD loves the righteous.
> The LORD watches over the strangers;
> he upholds the orphan and the widow.
>
> Psalm 146.7–9

Sometimes when I am discussing Christianity or religion with friends, they say that Christianity has been responsible for a great many terrible things in our history, such as the Crusades, the Spanish Inquisition and countless wars, just to name a few. I have to admit that most of these accusations are correct, but I can also point out that in a quiet unheralded way the adherents of different traditions and faiths have been doing good: monks and nuns, for example, have been tending the sick, feeding the poor and welcoming the stranger for centuries.

In our own day, if you go into any of our towns or cities where people seeking asylum have been sent, I will wager that it is the church groups that do most to help these strangers in whatever way they can. They are heeding the words of Jesus.

Recently I went to see a friend of mine who is an Anglican priest. When I knocked on his door it was opened, to my surprise, by a young olive-skinned man who greeted me with a smile. 'I am Jamal,' he said.

It turned out that Jamal was an Iraqi. My friend John told me he had come across Jamal huddled on a park bench. John sat down next to him and listened to his story. His application for permission to stay in this country had been turned down, because officials did not believe his story. The government had given orders that he was to be deported, and because he was certain he would be tortured or killed if he returned to Iraq, Jamal had run from his lodgings to the park where John had found him.

'When did you last have anything to eat?' John asked.

He took Jamal home, fed him and told him he could stay as long as he liked. No wonder Jamal was smiling.

The Christian Celts had a good understanding of how Jesus taught that we should treat the stranger:

> I saw a stranger yestreen.
> I put food in the eating place,
>   drink in the drinking place,
>   music in the listening place.
> And in the sacred name of the Triune
> he blessed me and my house,
>   my cattle and my dear ones.
> And the lark said in her song:
> 'Often, often, often,
>   goes the Christ in the stranger's guise.'

Not long after I had written this, I received an email from my friend Vivien, together with photographs of two children. The message read as follows:

To all who can help:

These are photographs of Sagara junior and Aloka that I took just this last Sunday. Two days later on Tuesday at 6.30 a.m. the family were woken by eight state officials (at 6 a.m. their lawyer had received a fax stating that their appeal for asylum had been rejected). Their parents Geetha and Sagara were placed in separate rooms away from their children who were then woken and dressed by social workers. Their mother, Geetha, suffered a seizure and temporary paralysis down her side. In this condition she was dragged downstairs. The family were then taken in a van to the Yarlswood Detention Centre in Bedford, where they are behind bars awaiting deportation to Colombo, Sri Lanka, this Saturday at 10.45 a.m.

Their many friends are trying a desperate last-ditch attempt to appeal for a High Court Order to stop deportation.

Viv then included the following message from a small group of people trying to support this family:

We understand that sometimes it might seem like there's nothing we can do about the growing levels of violence and unrest that seem to be surrounding more and more of us as the years pass by. However, by writing a letter of support you will be helping an innocent family cling to the peace and security that they have found here in this country.

We cannot change events that have already taken place, that's in the past, but we can change how we react to them in the future and we can make the ultimate difference to the life of any family in great trouble by supporting their basic human rights to live a peaceful and untroubled life.

For this family we are as a community of friends living proof that the loving support and friendship of a community can heal the wounds caused by unspeakable physical, mental, emotional hardship and grief. We can together help them rebuild their lives and grow their roots even further in this community, giving opportunities to their children which they would not otherwise have.

I am writing this on Good Friday, having just returned from the Procession of Witness through the streets of our town, along with a hundred or so other Christians from various traditions. Last year, on this day, I walked in this same procession, trying to concentrate on the prayers and meditations that were read and the hymns that we sang, trying to focus on Jesus and his passion, but all the while grieving for my friend Mairi who had died in a house fire two doors away from me only a few hours earlier. It seemed to me then that the suffering of Mairi and the suffering of Jesus were somehow linked.

As I walked with friends from all the different churches this morning, my personal sorrow was not quite so intense, but again my thoughts and feelings were distracted. Someone read some words from Lamentations:

> Is it nothing to you, all you who pass by?
> Look and see
> if there is any sorrow like my sorrow . . .
>
> Lamentations 1.12

And I thought, every deep sorrow is like the sorrow of Jesus, and his tragic suffering was like the tragic suffering of all victims, because he was and is one of us in our humanity. It is pointless to try to measure one person's pain against another's, and we cannot make a fair comparison between the suffering of Jesus and that of other human beings. It is true that Jesus went through all sorts of anguish before his actual death. He was cruelly subjected to physical pain: when the crown of thorns was placed on his head, when he was flogged, when the nails tore through his flesh, when his body was stretched on the cross and he could scarcely breathe, when he cried out, 'I thirst.' He also had to endure mental and emotional agony: in Gethsemane when he pleaded in fear and his friends let him down, when Judas and then Peter betrayed him, when he was jeered at and mocked, when his friends deserted him, when he cried out in despair, when he understood the depth of his mother's grief. All this was terrible, but we all know of people who have suffered one tragedy after another in their lives.

This morning as I walked and prayed and sang about the crucifixion of Jesus, my thoughts, and my feelings too, kept turning to the Karunathilaka family. I only heard about their plight this week, and they still don't know whether or not they will be deported tomorrow. They have lived in Britain for nearly seven years, their young son and daughter were born here and they have become part of a community where they are happy and able to contribute to the welfare of others. If they have to return to Sri Lanka they will be in great danger, partly because one of the parents is Sri Lankan and the other Tamil. On this Good Friday I am thinking of them and praying for them. They are locked up in the Detention Centre at Yarlswood, afraid and unbearably tense, knowing that their future and possibly their lives depend on an impersonal decision by the Home Office.

A phone call came through at noon on Holy Saturday. The family have not been deported . . . yet.

I was naked and you clothed me

The people in our present developed world who need clothing will usually be the homeless, who may need blankets more than they need actual clothes, and especially refugees who often come from much hotter countries than our own and therefore feel the cold far more bitterly than we do.

There are people living among us who don't have even enough clothes to keep them warm, and yet there are many others who 'wouldn't be seen dead' in the same clothes twice, who feel it is essential to be dressed in the latest fashion and the latest colour. Shopping, which for many women means shopping for clothes, has become almost a religion.

Charity shops are a great blessing for people on low incomes, and most churches will at least know of a collection place for clothes to be given to refugees. We can be sure Sipiwe from Zimbabwe will be happy to receive a warm pink jumper even though the season's colour is purple!

When I think about Jesus and clothing I remember St Paul's letter to the Colossians. Here Paul speaks as the voice of Jesus, teaching us the way to live:

> As God's chosen ones, holy and beloved, clothe yourselves with compassion, kindness, humility, meekness, and patience. Bear with one another and, if anyone has a complaint against another, forgive each other; just as the Lord has forgiven you, so you also must forgive. Above all, clothe yourselves with love, which binds everything together in

perfect harmony. And let the peace of Christ rule in your hearts, to which indeed you were called in the one body. And be thankful. Let the word of Christ dwell in you richly; teach and admonish one another in all wisdom; and with gratitude in your hearts sing psalms, hymns, and spiritual songs to God. And whatever you do, in word or deed, do everything in the name of the Lord Jesus, giving thanks to God the Father through him.

Colossians 3.12–17

I was sick and you visited me

Jesus himself very often healed the sick, those who were ill in mind or body:

At sunset all those who had friends suffering from diseases of one kind or another brought them to him, and laying his hands on each he cured them.

Luke 4.40, New Jerusalem Bible

He also visited the sick at home:

While he was saying these things to them, suddenly a leader of the synagogue came in and knelt before him, saying, 'My daughter has just died; but come and lay your hand on her, and she will live.' And Jesus got up and followed him, with his disciples . . . When Jesus came to the leader's house and saw the flute-players and the crowd making a commotion, he said, 'Go away; for the girl is not dead but sleeping.' And they laughed at him. But when the crowd had been put outside, he went in and took her by the hand, and the girl got up. And the report of this spread throughout that district.

Matthew 9.18–19, 23–26

Glenda

Glenda was my friend. She was a lot older than me, a widow and childless. She had always had a host of friends, but by now most of those of her own age had died.

Glenda was a humble woman who always kept busy. Every day she went to our local small hospital to visit the sick. As well as being kind, she was invariably cheerful, and she made sure that nobody in the hospital went without a visitor for more than a day.

In the town Glenda was very well liked; some people called her a saint, others an angel. If she had known about this, Glenda would have laughed her loud guffaw and said, 'They're talking nonsense! I'm only doing what Jesus told us to do in the Bible. Anyway, I love it!'

Then, very suddenly, Glenda herself became seriously ill and was taken into hospital. I was shocked to hear this and resolved to go and visit her the following day. But I didn't manage it; I was too busy. The next day some friends came round so I put my visit off again. On the third day I went round to the hospital with a bunch of flowers and a box of chocolates.

As I approached the ward a staff nurse came out. I asked if it would be all right to see Glenda. Then I noticed the tears in her eyes.

'I'm sorry,' she said. 'Glenda died this morning.'

I was in prison and you came to see me

Near the beginning of his ministry, when Jesus was in the synagogue at Nazareth, he stood up to read and unrolling the scroll, chose to read this passage from Isaiah:

> The Spirit of the Lord is upon me,
> because he has anointed me

to bring good news to the poor.
He has sent me *to proclaim release to the captives*
and recovery of sight to the blind,
to let the oppressed go free,
to proclaim the year of the Lord's favour.

Luke 4.18–19

It is a terrible thing to be in prison. Sometimes people who have never been inside a gaol are very scathing about all the amenities they imagine prisoners enjoy. For the most part they are wrong. Prisoners have lost their freedom, they are locked away from their families and friends, and they are at the mercy of their fellow inmates who may or may not be cruel. Prison is far from being a 'jolly'.

I believe that people who are a danger to society should be kept in secure accommodation for life, but I also think it is outrageous to go on building more and more prisons, because not only do prisons *not* work, but they are often inhumane institutions. It is important to bear in mind that two-thirds of all prisoners have committed drug-related crimes, while an alarming number suffer from mental health problems. Among women prisoners, a considerable proportion are guilty of petty offences such as failure to pay their fines. Surely in a civilized society these people do not need to be deprived of their freedom. What they do need is to be helped and rehabilitated.

When we visit people in prison we come to realize these truths. For those 'inside' it may be that the visits of friends or family are the only thing that keeps them sane.

Polly

I wish I could have a visitor. I don't care who, anyone would do. Best would be my mum, but she lives so far away and she's looking after my kids. She'd have to bring them with her, all the way by train, and I wouldn't want that. I don't want Gary and Mandy seeing the inside of this or any prison, not ever. I had their photos pinned on the cell wall next to my bed, but Samantha pulled them down and tore them into little bits in front of me. I don't even know what I'd done to annoy her, but I keep my head down when she's around.

It seems that everyone on this wing is having a visit this afternoon. Some of them have dolled themselves up – as much as you can, having to wear this outfit all the time, and Zoë asked to borrow my lipstick. I gave it to her; it's no use to me anyway. You can tell it's visiting time: there's a buzz around the place and everyone's on a high.

Not me, though. If only I could have just one visit it would help me through. The chaplain came once. He was nice, young, not much more than a boy. He asked me which denomination I belonged to, and when I said, 'Pardon?' because I didn't know what he was on about, he said, 'Sorry, which church do you attend?'

I said, 'None,' and I thought he would go then, but he sat down and asked me about my husband. I couldn't resist it: I said, 'None' again. He didn't seem fazed, so I told him about Gary who is four and Mandy who is two. I told him about Mum, too, how she's stood by me. Then it all came pouring out of me: what I'd done and why I'd done it and how I couldn't wait to get out of this hellhole. I even got started on all the things I miss, from the feel of the wind on my face to marshmallows!

I don't know what his religion is, but that priest or vicar or minister, whatever he is, is certainly a good listener. When he got up to go, I wanted to say, 'Please come to see me again,' but it didn't seem right, me not being religious at all.

Now I wish I had. I wish it so badly.

*   *   *

The passion of Jesus

As we meditate on the passion and death of Jesus, I think it's essential to remember that he endured everything as a human being: each painful experience was as cruelly felt as we would have felt it. Of course Jesus was different from us, radically different because he was, and is, God, but while he was alive as a man he lived every aspect of his life in a fully human way. The Second Vatican Council of the Roman Catholic Church expressed this in its last document, *Gaudium et Spes*, stating that Jesus 'worked with human hands, thought with a human mind, acted by human choice and loved with a human heart'. We might add 'suffered in human weakness'.

The word 'passion', used in relation to the end of Jesus' life, means suffering. It is not possible to know the precise point at which his suffering began. Most people have to suffer at some time or other, to a greater or lesser degree, and many who ordinarily appear cheerful and untroubled on the surface carry a weight of sorrow within them: the death of a child, for instance, or the pain of divorce, or the knowledge of a fatal illness.

Jesus must have experienced suffering from the beginning of his ministry, and probably earlier; he must have known he was destined to die a cruel death and often thought about it with dread. He used to leave the disciples to go off alone to pray, and we can imagine that in these times of solitude and special closeness to his Father he would have tried to face what was going to happen to him.

In the Gospel accounts, his 'official' suffering begins with his entry into Jerusalem in his last days.

> The Lord GOD helps me;
> therefore I have not been disgraced;
> therefore I have set my face like flint,

and I know that I shall not be put to shame;
he who vindicates me is near.

Isaiah 50.7–8

The passage from Isaiah refers to someone who is generally known as 'the suffering servant'. It is uncertain who the servant is but some scholars think Isaiah is prophesying the passion of Jesus. Whether or not this is true, I find the phrase 'I have set my face like flint' particularly moving, because I imagine Jesus did just that when he set foot in Jerusalem at the start of his last journey. Someone entering hospital to face a major operation, or a soldier going into battle for the first time, might well set their face like flint.

The Messiah enters Jerusalem

Then they brought it to Jesus; and after throwing their cloaks on the colt, they set Jesus on it. As he rode along, people kept spreading their cloaks on the road. As he was now approaching the path down from the Mount of Olives, the whole multitude of the disciples began to praise God joyfully with a loud voice for all the deeds of power that they had seen, saying,

Blessed is the king
who comes in the name of the Lord!
Peace in heaven,
and glory in the highest heaven!

Luke 19.35–38

We don't know why Jesus entered the city riding on a donkey. Perhaps it was to give him courage, to affirm what he had done, to reassure him that he was appreciated and loved.

I remember a time when I wrote and produced a play for a school. It was a great success, and after the last performance the leading lady was called on to the stage and given a bunch of lovely flowers amid enthusiastic applause. I was standing in the wings, hidden behind a curtain, waiting hopefully, but nobody called me on to the stage or gave me flowers.

At first I was hurt, then ashamed of my pride and self-centredness. I told a friend of mine about this, and he said, 'Don't be ashamed. You were right to be hurt. You deserved gratitude and praise. You are only human, after all.'

We sometimes forget that Jesus was, if not 'only' human, at least fully human. Surely he needed the acclamation of his people to help him face the coming days.

Gethsemane

They went to a place called Gethsemane; and he said to his disciples, 'Sit here while I pray.' He took with him Peter and James and John, and began to be distressed and agitated. And he said to them, 'I am deeply grieved, even to death; remain here, and keep awake.' And going a little farther, he threw himself on the ground and prayed that, if it were possible, the hour might pass from him. He said, 'Abba, Father, for you all things are possible; remove this cup from me; yet, not what I want, but what you want.' He came and found them sleeping; and he said to Peter, 'Simon, are you asleep? Could you not keep awake one hour? Keep awake and pray that you may not come into the time of trial; the spirit indeed is willing, but the flesh is weak.' And again he went away and prayed, saying the same words. And once more he came and found them sleeping, for their eyes were very heavy; and they did not know what to say to him. He came a third time and said to them, 'Are you still sleeping and taking your rest? Enough! The hour has come; the Son of Man is betrayed into the hands of sinners. Get up, let us be going. See, my betrayer is at hand.'

Mark 14.32–42

Four days after his joyful procession through the streets, Jesus took his last meal with his disciples. Afterwards, taking Peter, James and John with him, he went to the garden of Gethsemane, a beautiful peaceful place just outside the city walls, and there he prayed with fervent intensity. There can be no mistake about it: Jesus was terribly afraid. At this last moment he was looking for a way out, but his deep trust in his Father made him accept his destiny. The bravest people are always those who are most afraid, but still do what they have to do.

When he prays this most passionate prayer, Jesus addresses God as Abba, underlining the intimacy of their relationship.

In this fearful situation, Jesus was depending on the support of his friends. He didn't ask them to stand with him, to listen to his pleading, only to be there, to be a presence for him. When he found them all asleep, not once but three times, in spite of his begging them to stay awake, his misery deepened.

In times of great distress, it makes a huge difference to have someone standing by us, holding our hand or just being a silent presence. I am acutely aware of this because two years ago my sister, who lives at the other end of the country, had a massive stroke. Since then she has been unable to speak or move her limbs. She is fed artificially through a tube. No one knows how much, if anything, she can understand. But all this time, day after day, for several hours each day, her friend visits her, sits by her bed, talks to her, reads to her, holds her hand, strokes her face.

When Jesus came back to his disciples, after praying so earnestly, he found his friends asleep. Clearly they were quite unaware that he was going through such anguish, and their indifference must have made him feel very much alone in his distress.

In present-day Western society, loneliness is a terrible scourge and largely unrecognized. More and more people live on their own, a good many of them fulfilled and happy, but others shut away from any real friendship.

Colette was very happily married to Frank. People remarked on their closeness and smiled to see them walking hand-in-hand even in old age. They went everywhere together, did everything together. Then one night Frank had a heart attack and died.

They had no children, and Colette's only sister had also died. Her neighbours were kind but led busy lives. At first Colette made efforts to go out and mix with people, but one day she accidentally overheard two women talking about her.

'I was going to invite Colette,' said one, 'but you know what she's like, she never stops talking.'

'I know,' said the other woman, 'and it wouldn't be so bad if she had anything interesting to say. She's such a dull little woman.'

After that, Colette didn't go out, except to the shops. She stayed at home feeling more and more lonely, more and more miserable, but always with an ear cocked in case someone came knocking at her door. She had long given up hope that anyone would come to visit her when, one afternoon, she was startled by a ring on her doorbell. With more than a little anxiety, Colette went to answer it, telling herself it was probably someone collecting for charity or trying to sell her something.

When she opened the door, she recognized a woman she had known slightly in her church-going days. Colette felt reassured, she had liked Hilda; but then she felt panicky in case the woman had come to put pressure on her to go back to church. She managed to force a smile and invited Hilda into the house. They sat down and Hilda accepted a cup of tea. Then just as Colette was beginning to relax, she said, 'Well, Colette, I won't beat about the bush. I expect you're as busy as the rest of us, and I don't want to waste your time. But I've come to ask you a favour.'

Colette began to panic again, but Hilda went on, 'Do you know Mrs Wharton – Brenda?'

Colette shook her head. 'Well,' Hilda continued, 'she's a lovely woman and lives just a few doors away down this street. She had a bad fall in the summer, and now she's confined to a wheelchair. She's dreadfully lonely, Colette, and I wondered if you could spare the time to visit her – just occasionally, of course. I'm sure having someone like you to talk to would make all the difference to Brenda. I know it's a lot to ask, but do you think you could manage it?' Hilda paused. 'Loneliness is such a terrible thing, isn't it?' she said.

Then he withdrew from them about a stone's throw, knelt down, and prayed, 'Father, if you are willing, remove this cup from me; yet, not my will but yours be done.' Then an angel from heaven appeared to him and gave him strength. In his anguish he prayed more earnestly, and his sweat became like great drops of blood falling down on the ground.

Luke 22.41–44

Luke's account of the 'Agony in the Garden' as it is sometimes called, differs from Mark's and Matthew's. There is a note in the New Jerusalem Bible, commenting on the description of Jesus sweating. Apparently at one time these words were left out of the text. The note states: 'Their omission is explained by concern to avoid a humiliation which seemed too human.' Jesus was not too human, but he was very human; he sweated and bled and wept like the rest of us.

While he was still speaking, suddenly a crowd came, and the one called Judas, one of the twelve, was leading them. He approached Jesus to kiss him; but Jesus said to him, 'Judas, is it with a kiss that you are betraying the Son of Man?' When those who were around him saw what was coming, they asked, 'Lord, should we strike with the sword?' Then one of them struck the slave of the high priest and cut off his right ear. But Jesus said, 'No more of this!' And he touched his ear and healed him. Then Jesus said to the chief priests, the officers of the temple police, and the elders who had come for him, 'Have you come out with swords and clubs as if I were a bandit? When I was with you day after day in the temple, you did not lay hands on me. But this is your hour, and the power of darkness!'

Luke 22.47–53

Jesus has no time to recover from his ordeal in the garden when a gang of soldiers appears to arrest him. We can imagine the pain that the kiss of Judas gives him, but Jesus is strong now. Although he is the one being arrested, somehow he seems to be in control of the situation. He is quick to reprimand the disciple who cut off a soldier's ear: he will not tolerate violence or injustice even though the disciple was acting on his behalf. And he is not afraid to challenge his captors: we can see him standing up and looking them straight in the eye.

I went, just once, to Greenham Common, when the women's protest was in full swing. I like to think I would have gone more often, and perhaps even stayed there a while, but at the time I had a young family who were my priority. The women at Greenham were unafraid; they would look anyone in the eye, and they endured long-term physical deprivation in terms of food and warmth and comfort. Two of them invited me into their patch and gave me a mug of tea. It was easily the dirtiest cup that in my long life I have ever seen, but I saw they had no washing facilities and so – this was my contribution of courage – I drank it. In the face of loneliness and fear and distress, Jesus went through with what he had to do because he believed it was right. The women of Greenham, in spite of hunger, cold, discomfort and separation from loved ones, persevered with what they had to do because they believed it was right.

Some Christians, especially Roman Catholics, like to remember Christ's suffering by 'doing' the Way of the Cross. This means concentrating one at a time on the events (Stations) that led up to the crucifixion, and meditating on them.

This can be a powerful way of coming close to Jesus: to be, as it were, in solidarity with him, and also sometimes to relate his suffering to that of ordinary people.

This section of the book will be a Way of the Cross which I hope will help us to meditate on Jesus and learn to understand him more.

The first station:
Jesus is condemned to death

Pilate, wanting to release Jesus, addressed them again; but they kept shouting, 'Crucify, crucify him!' A third time he said to them, 'Why, what evil has he done? I have found in him no ground for the sentence of death; I will therefore have him flogged and then release him.' But they kept urgently demanding with loud shouts that he should be crucified; and their voices prevailed. So Pilate gave his verdict that their demand should be granted. He released the man they asked for, the one who had been put in prison for insurrection and murder, and he handed Jesus over as they wished.

Luke 23.20–25

Jesus had been pushed around, from the Sanhedrin to Pilate to Herod, then back to Pilate. He had been jeered at and cruelly mocked. When he heard the crowds baying for his life, shouting, 'Crucify him! Crucify him!' he must have remembered how only a few days earlier the crowds (some of them perhaps the same people) had strewn palms beneath his feet and shouted, 'Hosanna! Hosanna!' in his honour.

What a dreadful moment it was when he knew there was no hope left: he was condemned to die. And how must that moment be for the thousands of people in the USA who are condemned, not only to death, but also to many years of grim suffering on Death Row?

I think of Sally Clark, a solicitor and mother. When she found her much-loved baby dead, for no apparent reason, how must she have felt? Only one of my babies died, and I know what that was like, but then Sally had a second little boy and he died too, also of a cot death as it later transpired. But meanwhile, police came to Sally's house and arrested her. She was charged with the murder of her two sons and sent for trial. It is impossible for me, and I guess for most people, to imagine what Sally felt when she heard the jury's verdict: 'Guilty.' Impossible to imagine too what horrors awaited Sally when she arrived in prison as a child-murderer. Subsequently after years in prison she was found to have suffered a miscarriage of justice, and released. But only God knows what the state of her mind was then.

Very sadly, Sally died only a few months ago, still relatively young.

Dear Lord Jesus, you know what it is like to be condemned to death. We pray for all those who have to stand trial and await the jury's verdict, especially the innocent. We pray for those in prison, that they may be free from harm and able to use their time to good advantage. We pray for all parents whose children have died. Amen.

The second station:
Jesus is crowned with thorns

Then the soldiers of the governor took Jesus into the governor's headquarters, and they gathered the whole cohort around him. They stripped him and put a scarlet robe on him, and after twisting some thorns into a crown, they put it on his head. They put a reed in his right hand and knelt before him and mocked him, saying, 'Hail, King of the Jews!' They spat on him, and took the reed and struck him on the head. After mocking him, they stripped him of the robe and put his own clothes on him. Then they led him away to crucify him.

Matthew 27.27–31

Now Christ's journey to the cross has begun. Isn't it enough that he is going to die? Not for the soldiers, bullies like the thugs who roam our streets today, mugging old women and stabbing children to death. But these soldiers are worse than that: they are having fun. They are inventing all the ways to torture him that they can think of. Where does this cruelty come from? Sadly, we start very young to mock anyone who stands out as different, particularly if they are weak, an easy target. Children who are fat, or wear glasses, or have a different accent, an unusual name: all are easy targets. And, like Jesus, they are defenceless. Like him, they cannot fight back, they are stripped of their dignity, the butt of cruel laughter.

Over twenty years ago, and I fervently hope things have improved since then, a friend of mine who worked in the police force told me this true story. A big, burly chap, obviously a working man, was arrested for being on a bus without a bus pass. He was taken to the police station, and for some reason told to strip. Under his rough workman's clothes he was wearing women's underwear.

When the hoots of jeers and laughter had died down, he was made to stand as he was, so that each time different officers came in the mockery could start afresh.

Dear Lord Jesus, it is horrible to think of the indignities that you, the King of Kings, had to endure. I pray for all victims of bullying, whether verbal or physical, and I pray also for the bullies, that their hearts may be changed, that they may see and understand the effects of their cruelty. Amen.

The third station:
Jesus falls

As they led him away, they seized a man, Simon of Cyrene, who was coming from the country, and they laid the cross on him, and made him carry it behind Jesus.

Luke 23.26

In the Gospels there is no mention of Jesus falling, but there is a long tradition that he fell three times on his way to be crucified. It does seem likely, after the flogging and other torturing that he had received, that he was too weak to carry his cross on his own, and so stumbled and fell. That may have been why the soldiers, perhaps in a hurry to get the whole thing over, got someone from the crowd to carry the cross for him. How would that have made Jesus feel? Humiliated? Grateful? Ashamed? Perhaps he was already beyond caring what happened to him. And what about Simon? Did he have a choice? Was he a godsend or an embarrassment? Was he touched and changed by his encounter with Jesus?

I had the privilege of working in a school where all the children were, by definition, weak. Every one of them was in some way disabled: deaf, blind, suffering from spina bifida or cerebral palsy, struggling with learning difficulties. One thing I learned from these children is that the strong are not superior to the weak and those who give are no better than those who receive. I think especially of Teresa, Teresa and me.

She was a severe case of cerebral palsy. She lived her life strapped tight in a tall wheelchair because the only part of her body that she could control was her left foot. She couldn't feed herself and the noises she struggled to make as speech were hardly intelligible.

I, on the other hand, was a teacher. I was healthy and strong, I had a full and happy life. I was very sorry that Teresa was so handicapped, but very glad to know her. After years of being locked in near silence, she learnt through the wonders of technology to type, using her left foot to control the machine. Now she could communicate at last. Teresa lost no time in revealing her bright personality to the world that was our school. We became friends, rather than pupil and teacher, and she used to laugh at me. We learnt from each other.

Dear Lord Jesus, to us living so long afterwards, it feels good to think you had some help on your way to Calvary, someone who wasn't mocking or hurting you. And we are glad for Simon who was given this chance to be so close to you. We pray for those who are weak, that they will have the courage to accept their frailty. We pray also for those who carry the burdens of the weak, those who work with the homeless, with refugees, with victims of torture, people with AIDS, and people with learning difficulties. Amen.

The fourth station:
Jesus meets the daughters of Jerusalem

A great number of the people followed him, and among them were women who were beating their breasts and wailing for him. But Jesus turned to them and said, 'Daughters of

Jerusalem, do not weep for me, but weep for yourselves and for your children.'

Luke 23.27–28

We know that some noble women of Jerusalem used to give soothing drinks to condemned criminals. It seems likely that many of the women who had supported Jesus in his ministry would have joined these in wanting to be present and witness his last hours as he struggled along the road towards his death.

DAUGHTERS OF JERUSALEM

We are the daughters of Jerusalem.
We were there – how could we not be there? –
in solidarity with Jesus.
We stood with our sisters from Jericho,
from Nazareth, Capernaum, Bethsaida,
and all the places we have walked with him.
I sometimes washed his tunic,
I mended the tears in his cloak.
When he was hungry I gave him bread and honey,
when he was thirsty I gave him water and sometimes
    wine,
when he seemed lonely I tried to comfort him.
I watched him walk away, into the hills to pray.
We listened to his teachings and saw his healings,
we laughed with him, we cried with him,
we prayed with him.

And then we came together
to be there for him in that time of tribulation.
We didn't think he'd notice us
with so many people pressing round

jeering and mocking him.
But he lifted his head
and we saw his poor face, wet with blood and sweat.
He looked straight at us and began to speak
even that was painful for him.
He said, 'Daughters of Jerusalem, do not weep for me,
weep, rather, for yourselves and for your children.'
We should have known that even in this most pitiful
    situation,
he would be thinking, not of himself, but of us.

As we neared the place of crucifixion
we hung back a little,
respecting his mother and his closest friends.
It was their terrible privilege to stand under his cross.
But, for once in our lives, we women refused to obey
    him.
We carried on weeping, not for ourselves, but for him.

Jesus prophesied that terrible things would befall his beloved city.
What does he think about Jerusalem now? It is a city torn apart by
violence and division. Young men with grim faces, scarcely out of
their teens, guard the city gates, holding weapons that seem too
big for them. Psalm 122 was written in praise of Jerusalem, and
ends with these lines:

> Pray for the peace of Jerusalem:
> 'May they prosper who love you.
> Peace be within your walls,
> and security within your towers.'
> For the sake of my relatives and friends
> I will say, 'Peace be within you.'
> For the sake of the house of the LORD our God,
> I will seek your good.

Sadly, to the watching world, Jerusalem today appears as a symbol of violence.

Let us pray for the peace of Jerusalem.

The fifth station:
Jesus is nailed to the cross

As they drive in the nails,
the pain and the fear are intense.
Jesus lies helpless, trapped.
There is no escape now
and already he can guess how it will be.
Will he be able to bear the agony?

It is the question that haunts prisoners of
    conscience,
'If I am tortured,
will I be able to bear the agony?
Will I be able to keep silent
when I am commanded
to betray my friends?'

Victims of torture
recover very slowly
if they recover at all.
They need understanding,
patience and healing
for the bodies bruised and bleeding,
minds bewildered and afraid,
spirits broken.

Jesus is the victim now,
the tortured one.
His body is battered,
exhausted,
his spirit faint.
No one can help him.
He has no choice but to submit to death.

It is terrible to think of the intensity of Christ's suffering when he was nailed to the cross. When someone we love is in pain we feel at our wits' end, longing to find some way to take away the anguish, wishing the pain could be ours instead. So it must have been for Mary.

I remember how it was when one of my children was very ill and too young to understand what was happening to him. He was crying with pain and all I could do was hold him and try to murmur soothing words. I felt helpless.

Lord Jesus, you were helpless when you lay on your cross and the cruel nails were hammered into your flesh. We trust that now you are with all who suffer in the heart of their pain. Amen.

The sixth station:
Jesus speaks to his mother

Jesus feels forsaken.
He can no longer sense
the presence of his Father.
He is frightened, rejected, in terrible pain.
In these last moments
he feels alone in all the world
until he looks down

and sees his mother standing there
and knows that love enfolds him,
even now.
He answers that unswerving, selfless love,
that suffers with and for him,
with his own selflessness
and tender care for her.
He looks down from the cross
on Mary and the other faithful ones:
and John, the disciple he loved so well.
They stand firm together,
focused in silence on his suffering,
and Jesus says, indicating John,
'Woman, behold your son.'

Even his mother,
for all her courage,
needed support and protection,
needed love.

In a vast refugee camp in Darfur
the many orphaned children
sit in rows, listless and numb,
their eyes, once beautiful,
now dull, without expression,
needing, beyond anything else,
someone to love them.

They have been subjected
to terror and disease,
to near-starvation.
They are safe now,
fed and clothed,
their bodies healed.

But there is no one left
who loves them
as a mother loves her child.

We may wonder how Mary felt when Jesus asked John to take care of her. It seems likely that she respected John, and perhaps loved him because she would know that Jesus loved him. But I think that, in that moment, she would have wanted no one except her son. No one else would come near him in his mother's eyes. And I think that John might have felt differently. He would be honoured that he was the one chosen to take care of Mary, although he too would only have been focused on one person, his Master and friend, hanging there on the cross.

Lord Jesus, I pray that my home will always be a place of welcome to all who come there. Amen.

The seventh station:
Jesus dies

Jesus is dying,
hanging on that cross,
upheld not by the cruel nails
but by his own great love
for all humanity.
He is brother to all who suffer,
friend to every victim.
He is one with the tortured, with the lonely,
with refugees and all who are afraid.
In this moment,
he is one with his mother
who stands,
her soul pierced by the sword,

and goes on standing.
He is one with the criminal hanging nearby,
one even with Judas Iscariot
who betrayed him
and now knows the blackest despair.
In empathy, in agony,
the Son of God is crucified.

He is one with the young man
dying of AIDS
in a hospital in Uganda.
He is dying alone,
his parents and brother
already dead
from the same disease.
He is tormented,
bewildered,
afraid,
in pain.

For all our faith in the after-life, our belief that we will be united with God, there is a terrible finality about death which the disciples, confused and disappointed, must have felt. And as happens so often in ordinary lives, the searing anguish of Mary and the others standing with her must have been tempered by an enormous sense of relief that his dreadful ordeal was ended.

Lord Jesus, with a full heart I thank you for everything you have done and continue to do in our lives. Amen.

The last words of Jesus

It can be quite confusing to read the accounts of Christ's death in the Gospels, because they differ so much in detail. Jesus spoke very few words from the cross; indeed, it must have been a terrible struggle for him to speak at all because of the way he had to hang there. But it is worth looking at the words recorded by each of the evangelists.

> When it was noon, darkness came over the whole land until three in the afternoon. At three o'clock Jesus cried out with a loud voice, 'Eloi, Eloi, lema sabacthani?' which means, 'My God, my God, why have you forsaken me?' When some of the bystanders heard it, they said, 'Listen, he is calling for Elijah.' And someone ran, filled a sponge with sour wine, put it on a stick, and gave it to him to drink, saying, 'Wait, let us see whether Elijah will come to take him down.' Then Jesus gave a loud cry and breathed his last.
>
> Mark 15.33–37

Mark's and Matthew's accounts are very similar, and at this point almost identical. Unlike Luke and John, they tell us that Jesus quoted this first line of Psalm 22. Some people, not wishing to admit that he came so close to despair, point out that the psalm ends on a more upbeat note and suggest that Jesus had this in mind. It seems more likely to me that this was indeed a spontaneous cry of desolation; that in those moments the humanity of Jesus superseded his divinity, that he felt utterly abandoned and alone. And that last loud cry he gave as he breathed his last breath: what could be more human than that?

It is not, thank God, a common experience to feel completely abandoned, but perhaps such instances of desolation occur more frequently than we realize. Last year in Eritrea, Helen, a young woman who was a gospel singer, was thrown into a shipping container and told she would stay there until she agreed to renounce her Christian faith. She was alone at the bottom of this great box from where there was no escape. By night the cold was unbearable, and by day the heat, beating on the metal walls of the container, likewise. Helen must have felt like crying out 'My God, my God, why have you forsaken me?' But she refused to give up her faith and eventually, probably through the work of Amnesty International, she was released.

Helen's is a true story; what happens to many children in Zimbabwe is also true. Those of us who live in the safety and comfort of the Western world can hardly begin to imagine what it is like for a young girl to be snatched from her family and taken to join the army of child soldiers. On her very first night, she and the other newly captured girls are raped. Surely such a child would want to echo the desolate cry of Jesus from his cross?

Luke tells the same story rather differently. He has Jesus speaking twice, with quite different words:

When they came to the place that is called The Skull, they crucified Jesus there with the criminals, one on his right and one on his left. Then Jesus said, 'Father, forgive them; for they do not know what they are doing.'

Luke 23.33–34

The capacity of Jesus to forgive in such a situation and while his torture was continuing stretches our credulity to the limit. He is showing himself to be like his Father: full of compassion, able to love without condition, to love even those who are treating him with such remorseless cruelty.

But if we find his ability to forgive almost beyond belief, how do we react to the extraordinary compassion of Mrs Walker? She is a humble black woman who, because of her unwavering faith in God, brought herself to forgive the young men who with an axe killed her son Anthony, the son she loved so much, simply because of the colour of his skin. When asked how she managed to do this, she said, 'Jesus forgave those who crucified him, and I must try to follow him.' There is nothing pretentious about Mrs Walker; she was not showing off or trying to impress anyone. She simply did what she believed to be right.

A little further on in his account of the crucifixion, Luke tells the story of the two thieves hanging on either side of Jesus.

> One of the criminals who were hanged there kept deriding him and saying, 'Are you not the Messiah? Save yourself and us!' But the other rebuked him, saying, 'Do you not fear God, since you are under the same sentence of condemnation? And we indeed have been condemned justly, for we are getting what we deserve for our deeds, but this man has done nothing wrong.' Then he said, 'Jesus, remember me when you come into your kingdom.' He replied, 'Truly, I tell you, today you will be with me in Paradise.'
>
> Luke 23.39–43

Jesus is showing more mercy, more forgiveness. We have just tried to imagine what it was like for a young girl to be faced with absolute horror; now we can try to imagine what it was like for a man to receive the promise of joy beyond anything he might have hoped or dreamed of.

There are a lot of things we don't know about the crucifixion. We cannot be sure who exactly stood at the foot of the cross, apart from those who are named. But I wonder if Mary was not the only mother who witnessed her son's cruel death that day?

SOMEONE'S SON

Nobody knew my name;
nobody does now.
I've always lived in the shadows

since I ran away.
I just couldn't stand it any more
so I ran, and the worst thing,
the worst thing any mother can do:
I left my child with him, the brute.

I wasn't surprised when Dismas, the boy,
grew up like his father.
I wasn't surprised when I heard
that he would be crucified.
I had hardened my heart against him,
but when I saw the mother
of the man they call Jesus
standing at the foot of his cross,
it suddenly struck me:
I could do that too.

All I had ever done for my son
was abandon him,
and now, at the very last moment,
I had this chance:
to do something for him,
something for love.

It didn't work out that way of course.
I fixed my eyes on him
willing him to look down and see me,
and know I was his mother,
but he never did.
Standing there, shivering and dry-eyed,
so close to all those good people,
I heard my Dismas speaking.
And when the man Jesus said to him,

'Today you will be with me in Paradise',
suddenly it was all right.
I was all right,
not happy, not reconciled with my son,
and yet, at last, after all these years,
I was at peace.

I crept away,
nobody saw me,
nobody cared,
but my son, Dismas, was with God.

Indescribable joy, the sense of one's cup overflowing, only happens to us occasionally, and for some of us never. Often it comes, as with my friend Sarah, after years of unhappiness and struggle. Sarah had always wanted a baby; after seven miscarriages and several failed attempts at IVF, she and David her husband adopted two little boys. When the younger of these, Simon, was three, Sarah found that she was pregnant again. She expected a miscarriage or a stillbirth, and it was only in the moment when she held her newborn daughter, Jessie, in her arms that she felt a great surge of wonder and joy. This is what Jesus gave to the man we call 'the repentant thief' in his last moments.

It is perhaps rather ironic that John, who in his Gospel has Jesus speaking hundreds and hundreds of words, tell us of only six that he spoke as he was dying.

After this, when Jesus knew that all was now finished, he said (in order to fulfill the scripture), 'I am thirsty.' A jar full of sour wine was standing there. So they put a sponge full of the wine on a branch of hyssop and held it to his mouth. When Jesus had received the wine, he said, 'It is finished.' Then he bowed his head and gave up his spirit.

John 19.28–30

In some ways, Christ's words, 'I am thirsty' move me more than anything else he has said from the cross. They seem so like a simple plea for help such as anyone might make, and it is so sadly ironic that Jesus who said 'I am thirsty' had said to the Samaritan woman:

> Everyone who drinks of this water will be thirsty again, but those who drink of the water that I will give them will never be thirsty. The water that I will give will become in them a spring of water gushing up to eternal life.
>
> John 4.13–14

We cannot live without water. No one knows this better than the destitute children of the developing world. Crops cannot grow, flowers cannot bloom, our bodies cannot live without water; our souls need the water of life, the spirit of Jesus, to survive.

In Psalm 63 we read:

> O God, you are my God, I seek you,
> my soul thirsts for you;
> my flesh faints for you,
> as in a dry and weary land where there is no water.

As Jesus dies, he says, according to John, 'It is finished.' We take this to mean that he is acknowledging that the task he was sent on earth to do has now been accomplished. He speaks as the Son of God.

NICODEMUS

> It is so typical of me.
> I finally did it,
> brought myself to do something,
> and of course it was too late

Jesus was dead,
I was too late,
now nothing I could do was any use.
I know he loved me,
I know he knew me,
knew me for the coward that I was.
I went to see him once, by night,
under cover of dark.
I was afraid you see,
I wanted so much
to be accepted and respected
in the Sanhedrin.
I knew they wouldn't approve
if they found out
that I was, so to speak
consorting with the enemy.
But how could he, Jesus,
be anyone's enemy?
I never met anyone
so true, so brave,
so loving.
I like to think he was my friend.
We are all broken-hearted now,
united in the deepest sorrow,
but I bear such guilt too,
the guilt of cowardice.
I've brought him something,
too late, of course,
a mixture of myrrh and aloes,
a pathetic gift,
yes, pathetic, like me.
Yet I think, when he knows,
he will smile.

The Way of the Cross with Celine

We have just been meditating on the passion and death of Jesus, in a simple Way of the Cross. When I heard about Celine, I thought it might make an appropriate postscript to write the bare bones of her story as I learnt it from the Medical Foundation for the Victims of Torture. When we follow the events that took place in her young life, we feel much the same emotions as we do when we reflect on the last days of Jesus.

1999	Raped. Brother forced to rape her then murdered. Celine flees her home. Returns to protest at disappearing refugees.
2001	Arrested and detained for a month. Raped and sexually assaulted, repeatedly.
2004	Entire family murdered. Flees to UK. Placed in a hostel, Celine is kept awake by her room-mate's many male friends. This gives her flashbacks to her rape and abuse ordeals. Pregnant, poorly nourished, she is unable to sleep. Nightmares keep her awake vomiting with fear.
Christmas	She delivers her baby daughter, stillborn. This marks the onset of a new level of emotional crisis.
2005 April	Celine's Medical Foundation psychiatrist continues her treatment and the idea of a headstone for her baby is raised as a means to gain some peace. The Medical Foundation pays for her to take a short break in Dorset. This helps her progress.
2006 March	Celine is given refugee status and is thrown out of her emergency accommodation. Her Medical Foundation caseworker pressures the council's Homeless Persons unit to provide a place to live.

	With no income the Foundation's Relief Committee awards five payments so that she can buy food.
July	A funeral service and headstone are provided by the Relief Committee for her stillborn child. This is very upsetting but is the beginning of her accepting her loss and moving forward.
	The Council provides Celine with her own flat. This is the first time she has not been in shared accommodation since arriving in the UK. The flat is completely empty and, because she has no money, the Relief Committee helps her buy essentials. Joining the Women's Next Step Group, she is finally able to open up about her past experiences and the loss of her baby.
Christmas	Celine enrols at college.

Why have I told the story of Celine in a book about Jesus? I have told it because I see a parallel between his suffering and hers, because it shows not only human degradation at its worst, but also man's humanity to man in the work of the Medical Foundation. I have no idea whether Celine is a Christian, but I do believe that the Spirit of Jesus is alive in her amazing courage and perseverance.

Dear Lord, I pray for Celine, someone I will never meet but who inspires me with her story. I pray that she will be healed of her horrific wounds and that soon she will be able to enjoy happiness and fulfilment.

I pray also for all those like her, most of whom suffer undiscovered and cannot be saved from their predicament.

I pray too for the success of the work of the Medical Foundation for the Victims of Torture and for all people who do their utmost to help those who endure hardship and terror. Amen.

*   *   *

Resurrection stories

It can be quite confusing to try and make sense of the accounts of what happened to Jesus after the resurrection. He seems to have appeared in different places, at different times and to different people. He appeared when no one expected him, then suddenly vanished.

But if it is confusing for us, it must have been even more so for the evangelists. They would hear these marvellous stories passed down orally from generation to generation, perhaps embroidered a little here and there, or subtly altered.

And if it was confusing for the evangelists, it must have been even more so for the people who actually experienced these dramatic events, encounters with Jesus which shook them to the depths of their being and which they had difficulty in under-standing.

Yet however much these stories perplex us, they also move us deeply and give us greater insight into the wonderful human being who was also the Son of God.

When Jesus spoke Mary's name in the garden, we can sense the tenderness and compassion he felt for her, and we know that when we are anxious and distressed, we can turn to him who said:

Come to me all you that are weary and are carrying heavy burdens, and I will give you rest.

Matthew 11.28

But Mary stood weeping outside the tomb. As she wept, she bent over to look into the tomb; and she saw two angels in white, sitting where the body of Jesus had been lying, one at the head and the other at the feet. They said to her, 'Woman, why are you weeping?' She said to them, 'They have taken away my Lord, and I do not know where they have laid him.'

When she had said this, she turned round and saw Jesus standing there, but she did not know that it was Jesus. Jesus said to her, 'Woman, why are you weeping? For whom are you looking?' Supposing him to be the gardener, she said to him, 'Sir, if you have carried him away, tell me where you have laid him, and I will take him away.' Jesus said to her, 'Mary!' She turned and said to him in Hebrew, 'Rabbouni!' (which means Teacher). Jesus said to her, 'Do not hold on to me, because I have not yet ascended to the Father. But go to my brothers and say to them, "I am ascending to my Father and your Father, to my God and your God."'

John 20.11–17

MARY MAGDALENE

The night after he died I couldn't sleep.
I was distraught.
It was only after he'd gone, you see,
that I realized how much I loved him,
and understood, for the first time,
the depth of his love for me,
for all of us women and his disciples.
Jesus had no favourites,
but each of us was truly dear to him,
precious even.
I knew I could not live without him.
While it was still dark I ran down to the tomb.
I hardly knew what I was doing.
I think I took some spices to anoint his poor body,
forgetting the great stone blocking the entrance to the
    cave.
But to my astonishment, the stone was rolled away.
Stupid with grief, I began to cry till I pulled myself
    together

and looked inside the tomb.
He wasn't there!

There were two men dressed in white;
they must have been angels.
I was frantic now: I know I talked to them,
but I forget now what I said.
I turned round and saw another man.
He was not an angel; a gardener, I thought.
I began to cry again.
He spoke kindly, asking why I was weeping.
I mumbled something
and the next moment he spoke again.
He said, 'Mary!'
He said my name.
For a split second I stared at him.
Then I ran to him, Jesus, my Lord!
I was transported, in an instant,
from hell into heaven.

In John's account, we can only feel wonder that after his terrible ordeal Jesus could show such tenderness and affection for Mary, and speak to her with such apparent calm. Perhaps any one of us, man or woman, who believes in the resurrection, would have loved to be Mary Magdalene in that dramatic moment.

Doubting Thomas

I think that most people, reading how Thomas reacted when the disciples told him they had seen Jesus, would feel a certain warmth towards Thomas, an identification with him perhaps. To doubt, even to doubt our faith, is not sinful; it is normal. It is natural that as we grow in knowledge and love of God, all sorts of questions arise in our minds. The people of absolute rigid certainty whose minds are closed, who refuse to change or to listen to different viewpoints, these are further, I believe, from the Kingdom of God than the doubters whose hearts and minds are open.

And there is no doubt about the sincerity of Thomas when he comes face to face with the Risen Jesus.

But Thomas (who was called the Twin), one of the twelve, was not with them when Jesus came. So the other disciples told him, 'We have seen the Lord.' But he said to them, 'Unless I see the mark of his nails in his hands, and put my finger in the mark of the nails and my hand in his side, I will not believe.'

A week later his disciples were again in the house, and Thomas was with them. Although the doors were shut, Jesus came and stood among them and said, 'Peace be with you.' Then he said to Thomas, 'Put your finger here and see my hands. Reach out your hand and put it in my side. Do not doubt but believe.' Thomas answered him, 'My Lord and my God!'

John 20.24–28

THOMAS

When it happened I felt intense shame.
My face was burning.
I felt awe, too, such as I never felt before
at the wonder of his being here again,
at the wonder of his being here, surely,
not just as a man like us,
my friend and companion,
but the very Son of God!

Afterwards, when he had gone,
I sat alone, just pondering.
I thought how much I loved him.
Then it occurred to me
that he came back again, perhaps,
especially for me.
And I knew that my love for him
would never match his love for me.

The road to Emmaus

Now on that same day two of them were going to a village called Emmaus, about seven miles from Jerusalem, and talking with each other about all these things that had happened. While they were talking and discussing, Jesus himself came near and went with them, but their eyes were kept from recognizing him . . . As they came near the village to which they were going, he walked ahead as if he were going on. But they urged him strongly, saying, 'Stay with us, because it is almost evening and the day is now nearly over.' So he went in to stay with them. When he was at the table with them, he took bread, blessed and broke it, and gave it to them. Then their eyes were opened, and they recognized him; and he vanished from their sight. They said to each other, 'Were not our hearts burning within us while he was talking to us on the road, while he was opening the scriptures to us?'

Luke 24.13–16, 28–32

In some ways I find this the most puzzling of all the resurrection stories. Why didn't the two disciples recognize Jesus? Obviously, as they knew him to have been crucified, it would have been a huge shock to see him alive, but they must have known what he looked like, and even if he was wearing different clothing they must have known what his voice sounded like. Yet they walked a long way with him, listening to him intently and learning from him, without suspecting who he was. Then at the moment of Eucharist, of thanksgiving and sharing, they recognized Jesus. Perhaps these disciples were people like most of us, blind and deaf to what is really important, blind to the needs of the oppressed and the stranger, deaf to the cry of the poor.

AFTER THE JOURNEY

Cleopas was right.
Like his, my heart was burning within me
as we listened to him on the road.
We had been so cast down, both of us,
but somehow his words lifted us.
We saw things differently now;
we understood the scriptures
as we never had before.
We liked him; we wanted to hear more
and also to repay him with some hospitality.
So we were delighted when he agreed
to stop at this inn and share a meal with us.
I can't put into words the way I felt,
(nor can Cleopas, he tells me)
when his hands closed round the hunk of bread,
and looking gravely at each of us in turn,
he broke it.
We were both stunned.
I may have cried out,
and Cleopas reached for him,
but he was gone.
We weren't drunk; we weren't dreaming.

We knew this was real; we knew it was Jesus,
and we couldn't wait to tell the others:
'Jesus is alive!'

On the shore of Tiberias

John, easily the most meditative, profound and theological of the
evangelists, surprisingly ends his Gospel with an action-packed
drama, and shows us a Jesus so incontrovertibly human that he
cooks breakfast for his friends on the shore of the lake. There is
also a miracle, a snapshot of John, the perceptive one, and Peter,
the clown. Again, there is a Eucharist: Jesus steps forward and
gives his friends bread. At the end of the story, Peter is entrusted
with the pastoral care of the flock.

Just after daybreak, Jesus stood on the beach; but the disci-
ples did not know that it was Jesus. Jesus said to them,
'Children, you have no fish, have you?' They answered him,
'No.' He said to them, 'Cast the net to the right side of the
boat, and you will find some.' So they cast it, and now they
were not able to haul it in because there were so many fish.
That disciple whom Jesus loved said to Peter, 'It is the Lord!'
When Simon Peter heard that it was the Lord, he put on
some clothes, for he was naked, and jumped into the lake.
But the other disciples came in the boat, dragging the net full
of fish, for they were not far from the land, only a few hundred yards off.

When they had gone ashore, they saw a charcoal fire there,
with fish on it, and bread. Jesus said to them, 'Bring some of
the fish that you have just caught.' So Simon Peter went
aboard and hauled the net ashore, full of large fish, a
hundred and fifty-three of them; and though there were so
many, the net was not torn. Jesus said to them, 'Come and

have breakfast.' Now none of the disciples dared to ask him, 'Who are you?' because they knew it was the Lord. Jesus came and took the bread and gave it to them, and did the same with the fish. This was now the third time that Jesus appeared to the disciples after he was raised from the dead.

John 21.4–14

PHILIP

What a day that was!
Afterwards, I was tired out, but I couldn't sleep.
In my mind I went over and over what happened,
remembering all the details.
I didn't want to forget any of it.
There was a group of us: Simon, Thomas and Nathanael,
James, John, Jude and me.
Simon said, 'I'm going fishing' (he's the leader of our gang
and we usually do what he wants)
so we piled into the boat.
We stayed out all night, casting the net,
but we caught nothing.

It was beginning to get light,
when we noticed someone moving on the shore.
I thought it was odd, so early in the morning,
but he called out,
'Throw the net to starboard and you'll catch something.'
Simon shrugged. 'Might as well,' he said,
'just one more cast.'
I've never seen a net so full of fish;
it was too heavy to haul in.
Then John spoke (Simon may have been the boss,
but John was the thoughtful one, the one with intuition).

'It is the Lord!' he said.
Without a second's hesitation,
Simon snatched his cloak and pulling it around him,
jumped into the water.
I'll never understand him! Was he showing off?
Or was he just so eager to get to Jesus
because he was crazy about him?
We followed in the boat, dragging the net behind us.
Although there were so many fish, it didn't break.

Then the man on the shore said, 'Come and have breakfast!'
By now we all knew it was Jesus, but no one dared to say so,
not even Simon.

We were all cold and hungry after the long night.
The fish cooking on the fire smelled wonderful,
but when Jesus broke some bread and gave it to us,
for a moment I forgot my hunger. I remembered
the night before he died when we shared a meal together,
and he said, 'Do this in remembrance of me.'
I swear that whatever happens, I will never forget him.

After the meal Jesus took Simon to one side
and they spoke together for a while.
Simon came back looking strangely solemn
and from that moment on he seemed changed.
He didn't fool around any more,
he didn't act before he thought
and he asked us to call him 'Peter'.

*   *   *

Endpiece

As I come to the end of the book, I have been thinking more about the lovely image of the apple tree. By coincidence, my husband has just bought and planted a young apple tree in our garden. I went out to see it, and to my joy it was already blossoming. I went close to look at the flowers, and for the first time realized how perfectly beautiful they are. I thought how someone unknown, at some earlier time in history, had looked at Jesus as he or she knew him through the Gospels, and had seen an apple tree. I look at the apple tree in my garden, I see its perfection and its loveliness and I think of Jesus.

But delightful though this image is, I find that after reflecting on Jesus through these pages, the apple tree does not entirely satisfy me as an image for him. I have struggled, as perhaps the reader may do, to discover my own image for him, bearing in mind that, of course, no kind of image can ever adequately express or contain all that Jesus was and is.

It has turned out that I cannot come up with one single image, but there are three which affect me deeply. One is a woman in a photograph, not a specially dramatic one. She is shown picking over rubbish in a garbage dump. She is young and poorly dressed, wearing a headscarf, and looks, not sad or angry, but frighteningly resigned. For me she encapsulates suffering, the suffering caused by man's inhumanity to man, or in this case, to woman. She is an 'untouchable'. This is an image of Christ as victim.

My second image is more conventional. It is a shepherd, simple and strong, tending his lambs with passionate tenderness. He is love made real. So my second image of Christ is the good shepherd.

My third image is perhaps the most powerful one. It is light, light in all its various forms. It comes crushing every dark and evil thing, bringing life, bringing joy, bringing solace, fulfilling dreams, embracing everyone and everything, blessing the world and all its peoples. Jesus is the light of the world.

I would like to ask the reader: what is *your* image of Jesus Christ?

All through this book, I have been studying the Gospels, looking at Jesus, the man who walked the earth two thousand years ago in Palestine, trying to find out what sort of person he was. A lot of adjectives describe him: compassionate, courageous, just, gentle, astute, hard-working, prayerful, sensitive, truthful. But Jesus isn't only someone to be studied in Scripture, a wonderful person leading a memorable life, someone we remember because he was remarkable.

No, Jesus is far more than this: he is the Son of God and he is a presence in our lives, here and now. He is present when we are happy, enjoying the company of friends or the loveliness of creation; he is present when we struggle, when we are lonely, when our health begins to deteriorate. And if we can cultivate an awareness of Christ's presence all through our day, then we will become conscious of his abiding and unfailing love for us.

A RAINBOW-COLOURED CROSS
Personal prayers

RUTH ETCHELLS

'I don't know what to do, Lord. A lot of the time, I don't know what to do. Situations are rarely clear-cut, relationships are complex, demands are contradictory, choices are blurred. Which way to go? For whom give time – energy – money – attention – even prayer? [And then] you remind me of the simple rule: always to remove myself from the centre of [my] mindset, heart-set . . . and turn back to the joy of Christ being there instead.'

From *Third Day* – MORNING

A Rainbow-coloured Cross will provide comfort and affirmation for those experiencing the pain, struggle, freedom and joy of the Christian life. Richly imaginative, it offers morning and evening prayers for a month and represents the fruit of many years' daily conversation with God. A wide range of Christian writers are featured, including John Bell, Timothy Dudley- Smith, R. S. Thomas, Kathy Galloway, George Mac-Donald and Dag Hammarskjöld. However, almost all the material has been specially written for this book.

Those of us looking for a deeper spiritual life will be challenged, encouraged, surprised and reassured as we adopt this pattern of daily prayer. Those searching for new seasonal material will appreciate the supplementary section: here may be found prayers which give a wonderfully fresh perspective on Lent, Easter, Ascension Day, Pentecost and Trinity Sunday.

A Rainbow-coloured Cross is a companion volume to *Safer than a Known Way*, also published by SPCK. Each book may be read as complete in itself.

ISBN 978 0 281 05786 3

TEMPTATION AND TESTING

PAUL BUTLER

'I am faced with temptation on a very regular basis. Indeed there is a daily struggle with one temptation or another. Whether I am at my desk, out and about visiting community and church leaders, with my family at home or with friends, temptation keeps appearing . . . It has not lessened at all as I have grown older. It certainly has not lessened with the greater load of leadership to which God has called me over the years. Temptation simply is part of life, and will remain so until the day I die.'

From Chapter 3

Full of real-life stories and anecdotes, this refreshingly honest and liberating book tackles the enormously important subject of temptation and testing. It enables us to recognize how we are tempted, to explore why we so often choose not to do what we know is the right thing, and to encourage us to make positive choices.

Looking in turn at pairs of topics, such as worry and trust, money and contentment, violence and peace, sexual licence and sexual fidelity, the author draws frequently on Jesus' experience of being 'tempted in every way as we are'. As we begin to realize how wonderfully qualified – and how ready – Christ is to help us, we become more confident about handling the temptations that confront us. And through these tests, which expose us to the refining fire of God's love, we find ourselves growing more into the likeness of Jesus himself.

ISBN 978 0 281 05840 2

MEETING JESUS
Human responses to a yearning God

JEREMY DUFF AND JOANNA COLLICUTT McGRATH

Meeting Jesus explores the nature of encounter with God through reflecting on four key parables at the heart of Luke's Gospel:

- the lost sheep
- the lost coin
- the prodigal son
- the dishonest manager

The gospel accounts, which tell of many meetings between Jesus and individual people, speak at both a theological and a psychological level. The eternal meeting of God with humanity is played out in the world of human thought, feelings, actions and relationships. If we take the opportunity to participate in these parables, we will be struck by just how strong God's yearning is for us, 'his lost people'. We will also he able to explore the different ways in which human beings, in a range of circumstances, respond to God. We may even recognize something of ourselves and, through meeting with the Jesus of Luke's Gospel, come to encounter God afresh.

Anyone looking for a different, challenging and thought-provoking book on encountering God will profit from the fresh insights communicated here. *Meeting Jesus* will also be of value to clergy and those engaged in Christian ministry; students and others seeking to develop their theological thinking; and individuals with a particular interest in the relationship between human psychology and Christianity.

ISBN 978 0 281 05707 8

HOW TO BECOME A SAINT
A beginner's guide

JACK BERNARD

Those of us who frequently struggle in our lives as Christians may assume there's not much point in striving to become a saint. But as Jack Bernard argues persuasively in this life-enhancing book, we are all good candidates for sainthood because God deals exclusively with hopeless cases! Sainthood is, in fact, God's desire for every believer and available to anyone willing to embark on the journey to holiness.

'Provides a "back to basics" commonsense spirituality, which is much needed during this time of growing polarization among Christians. Sainthood, [Bernard] argues, is sorely misunderstood. It does not require perfection, but rather trust: trust in God and God's will, and trust in the goodness of oneself and others.'

Publishers Weekly

'Jack Bernard is the last person on earth to think of himself as a saint. This is why *How to Become a Saint* is so refreshing and so instructive. Here is a truly authentic, honest, down-to-earth word on what it means to be wholly undivided toward God. This book is neither a manual nor a manifesto; it is a wellspring of humble, hard-fought wisdom that can be applied by anyone who wants to love God more fully and faithfully.'

Charles Moore, editor of *Provocations: Spiritual Writings of Kierkegaard* and *Leo Tolstoy: Essential Spiritual Writings*

ISBN 978 0 281 05911 9

JOYFUL EXILES
Life in Christ on the dangerous edge of things

JAMES HOUSTON

'This book is the confessions of a life spent recklessly,' writes James Houston. It is certainly an engaging one, which draws on the author's college days in Edinburgh where he struggled with feelings of depression and dislocation; his time as a lecturer at Oxford when he met regularly with C. S. Lewis; and the visionary night-time experience that preceded the call to leave his professional career and native country to found Regent College, Vancouver – a graduate school of Christian studies, now with a world-class reputation. The author movingly conveys the central concerns of many years' teaching, writing and spiritual direction, exploring in turn:

- the breath of the hidden life
- being open to a visionary life before God
- the surrealism of Christian public life
- the journey towards becoming a person
- living the truth in love
- Christian transmission in an age of disjunction
- communal maturity in Christ

Having played a vital role in the restoration of spirituality to evangelicalism, there is no doubt that his wise volume will be a source of much challenge and stimulation – and comfort – to those of us seeking to be 'so taken over by Christ that we have a whole new identity defined by our encounter with him'.

'Be forewarned. This book is seriously countercultural! It presents not just a challenge to secular culture but more seriously a challenge to the comfortable ways we have shaped Christian culture. It is a call to embrace our identity as exiles and to live joyfully and prophetically from this place. It is a call to live on the edge, for it is there and only there that we can be truly open to God's presence in the world and the invitations to engagement with the world's problems and challenges.'

David G. Benner, author of *Desiring God's Will*

ISBN 978 0 281 05887 7

EMBRACING GRACE
A gospel for all of us

SCOT McKNIGHT

Don't just be saved by grace: *Live transformed* by grace.

According to evangelical theologian Scot McKnight, the gospel is too often reduced to forgiveness from sins and getting to heaven. The message of the Bible, and the story of God, is actually much bigger – and better – than just that. In *Embracing Grace*, the author presents an understanding of our relationship with Jesus that takes in the whole range of Scripture, from the original fall to the passion and resurrection of Christ.

'For too long, grace has been misunderstood as being nothing more than punishment avoidance. But God's grace was flourishing long before the first sin was ever committed. Scot McKnight, in his thoughtful and provocative way, helps us think again about the comprehensiveness of grace and the robust nature of the gospel. This is a book for people who want not only to be "saved" by grace, but to live by grace.'

John Ortberg

'Scot McKnight helps us see beyond various flat, one-dimensional partial gospels to a rich, multifaceted, textured, gracious gospel that embraces all the others . . . and all of us too. Highly recommended!'

Brian McLaren

ISBN 978 0 281 05959 1

BEAUTY AND BROKENNESS
Compassion and the Kingdom of God

MARTIN LLOYD WILLIAMS

In this beautifully written volume, Martin Lloyd Williams helps us explore the way we think about the relationship between creation and humanity. As we reflect on their respective beauty and brokenness, we are gently challenged to consider our understanding of compassion, to discern how we may fulfil our vocation as Christians to live truly compassionate lives.

The author uses as a starting point Mantegna's painting *Presentation at the Temple* which is, in many respects, a traditional Madonna and Child composition, except that the infant Jesus seems to be depicted as a child with Down's. It is as though Mantegna is suggesting that Jesus could have chosen to be born with a disability without its affecting the purpose of the incarnation.

How do we respond to this idea? Can we put on one side the notion that Jesus' purpose must primarily be defined in terms of a task to be achieved? If so, Martin Lloyd Williams argues, we might understand creation differently, recognizing instead a creator who recklessly throws himself into his creation because he cannot bear to be apart from it – a God who desires to elicit from us reciprocal love and fierce devotion. And what better way than to come among us as a person with learning impairments who, in worldly terms, could offer little if any return on the emotional investment we are making?

'I strongly recommend this book, with gratitude and renewed joy in all the riches God has showered upon us through loved ones who live with disability.'

The Revd Professor Frances Young, OBE

ISBN 978 0 281 05858 7

CREATIVE LOVE IN TOUGH TIMES

ANDREW CLITHEROW

The problem of evil and suffering is a black hole for many of us. It may seem difficult – even impossible – to pray to a God of love in the presence of so much pain. And the Church is not always helpful. Perhaps, Andrew Clitherow suggests in this prophetic book, it is time to lose the version of Christianity that Western consumerism has produced and to find a new way. Using insights from evolutionary theory, socio-biology and theology, he offers an accessible Christian spirituality which, centred in creative love, becomes a way of life.

'The history of the world is the history of the progress of love at the expense of evil.' In this exhilarating account of love's redeeming power, *Creative Love in Tough Times* urges us to rediscover the Christian faith – and to own it for ourselves.

'Andrew Clitherow's determination to be true to his experience and not to seek refuge in [his] prestigious role has led him to face some of the most intractable and painful obstacles to faith, and to emerge in love with a God whom he discovers in the centre of his own being . . . This book has the capacity to shake the foundations of those who may have grown complacent in their institutionalized security. For many, however, it will have the power to restore hope through its searing honesty and transparent vulnerability.'

Brian Thorne, Emeritus Professor of Counselling,
University of East Anglia and Lay Canon of Norwich Cathedral

ISBN 978 0 281 05885 3

WOUNDS THAT HEAL
Theology, imagination and health

EDITED BY JONATHAN BAXTER

In this invigorating volume, a variety of distinguished authors explore the interface between theology and health. Particular emphasis is placed on the role of the imagination within the Christian healing ministry, and how this makes an impact on and challenges current practice.

ROWAN WILLIAMS sets the tone by suggesting that theology is a story about healing, one that demonstrates 'how God transforms flesh . . . by creating living relationships with himself. ELIZABETH BAXTER reflects upon the healing journey as undertaken at Holy Rood House, Centre for Health and Pastoral Care. MARY GREY draws on her experience of breast cancer to describe what she calls the 'lost dimension' of the Christian healing ministry, 'ecomysticism'. CLIVE BARRETT demonstrates how a Judaeo-Christian understanding of peace is integral to the practice of Christian healing. HADDON WILLMER teases out the difference between forgiveness and healing in order to explore forgiveness 'in itself'. JONATHAN BAXTER, arguing from the perspective of an embodied spirituality, suggests that love, not health, should be the lens through which we interpret illness. ELAINE GRAHAM investigates the question of human identity and what it means to be 'post-human'. GRACE JANTZEN explores the tensional relationship between necrophilia and natality in the anchoritic spirituality of medieval mystical literature. PAUL AVIS reflects upon the Christian healing ministry through the 'indivisible trinity' of beauty, truth and goodness. ELIZABETH STUART, by way of exploring the sacrament of unction, speaks of the 'ever-broken heart of God' and, by analogy, of our own human experiences of suffering, illness and death. BRIAN THORNE, writing from the perspective of a person-centred therapist, develops the notion of 'spiritual intelligence' and its relevance for both secular and Christian healing ministries. JUNE BOYCE-TILLMAN explores the healing and reconciling power of music in our lives. ROGER GRAINGER writes about the role of drama, and specifically drama therapy, as a vehicle for personal and cultural healing. Finally, ANDREW SHANKS, through his translation of Hölderlin's poem 'Patmos', encourages us to face the sickness of our culture and ourselves with renewed verve and imagination.

ISBN 978 0 281 05830 3

CONTEMPLATIVE YOUTH MINISTRY

MARK YACONELLI

'Several years ago, the Christian Education team at St Andrew's Sunday school found itself floundering. We tried everything, especially prayer. But on bad days the classes were more like babysitting than Christian ministry. And just when we got to the end of our rope, our minister found out about Mark Yaconelli . . . He was teaching teachers how to be with kids in ways that helped them believe that church was a safe place . . . He was teaching children and teenagers how to be present with each other, and with God, in ordinary times, in the midst of messes, and during big and small triumphs. He was making God real, vital, fun, true.'

From the Foreword by Anne Lamott,
best-selling author of *Traveling Mercies*

Contemplative Youth Ministry is rooted in Mark Yaconelli's experience of co-directing the acclaimed Youth Ministry and Spirituality Project. Through this project, churches and youth ministers have explored contemplative prayer, discernment, spiritual direction, covenant community, spiritual practice and Sabbath-living as a way of resourcing ministries with youth. The results have been transformative, and this engaging book, richly illustrated with personal stories, provides refreshment and new ways of thinking for anyone who has grown weary or disillusioned with the vital tasks of working with and caring for young people.

ISBN 978 0 281 05782 5